The 106 Common Mistakes Homebuyers Make (and How to Avoid Them)

The 106 Common Mistakes Homebuyers Make (and How to Avoid Them)

Gary W. Eldred, Ph.D.

JOHN WILEY & SONS, INC.

New York • Chichester • Brisbane • Toronto • Singapore

Library of Congress Cataloging-in-Publication Data:

Gary W. Eldred, Ph.D.
    The 106 common mistakes homebuyers make: and how to avoid
them / by Gary W. Eldred.
        p. cm.
    Includes bibliographical references.
    ISBN 0-471-31191-X (paper: alk. paper)
    1. House buying.   I. Title.   II. Title: One hundred six most
common mistakes homebuyers make.
HD1379.E43 1994
643'.12—dc20   93-34163
                                                                    CIP

Printed in the United States of America

10 9 8 7 6 5 4 3

Introduction

Profit from the Mistakes of Others

Planning to buy a home? Good for you. Home ownership is one of the smartest personal and financial moves you can make—when you do it right. However, whether you are buying for the first time or the fifth time, there are many pitfalls to avoid and mistakes to prevent. And that's where this book can help. How? By helping you learn about the home-buying experiences of others. Here's the story of how this book came about.

Throughout the past 20 years I've taught college courses (graduate and undergraduate) in real estate; professional education programs for Realtors, home builders, and mortgage loan officers; and STOP RENTING NOW!™ seminars that are directed especially toward first-time homebuyers. From this teaching, I've found that one of the most favored classroom topics has been "How you can prevent mistakes in homebuying."

Although just about everyone knows that real estate, and particularly home ownership, stands out as one of the best ways to build personal wealth, a growing number of people now recognize that successful homebuying does not come automatically. It requires educated consumers. Shopping for a home and deciding to buy have become much more complex. There are many ways to go wrong. Naturally, then, learning about the mistakes of others has proved to be one of the best precautions to insure a happy and profitable home-buying experience.

When I first began to discuss mistakes in homebuying with my classes, I relied on many of my own experiences (and mistakes). Over time, though, I discovered students were eager to broaden their knowledge and learn firsthand about the mishaps, misfortunes, and mistakes suffered by others. As a result, I decided to incorporate "interview papers" into my class assignments. To carry out these assignments my students would interview Realtors, home builders, loan officers, and recent homebuyers.

The students would ask their interviewees to describe in concrete detail the home-buying (or real estate investing) mistakes that the interviewees had made themselves or had seen others make. Then the students would write up their conversations, submit them to me, and we would schedule a class session or two to discuss what the students had learned from their interviews and how they could profit by anticipating and preventing the mistakes they had learned about.

Because these classroom discussions proved quite popular and beneficial, many students suggested that they would like to see the most common (and costly) mistakes that I've collected brought together in a book. Fortunately, John Wiley & Sons, Inc., and senior editor Michael Hamilton agreed. In this book we've tried to help you benefit from the experiences of hundreds of persons who have been involved in home buying.

Many of the examples presented here have come from the interview papers written by my students. Others, however, are based on mistakes that I've seen made in some of the 100 or so real estate transactions in which I've been involved as a buyer, seller, or consultant. In addition, I've recounted some common experiences that I've read in magazines or newspaper articles. Of course, in many instances, to protect the privacy of individuals, I've changed names and specific identifying facts. But all told, these experiences are real. I truly believe that by reading through these examples and applying them to your own situation, you'll be able to make a better home-buying decision.

In an often-quoted passage the philosopher Santayana has written that those who fail to learn from the mistakes of the past are condemned to repeat them. My hope is that by reading through the mistakes and lessons illustrated throughout this book, you will be able to truly enjoy and profit from the home you buy.

Contents

Chapter 2   Your Home as an Investment   25

Chapter 5   **Comparing Homes**   **97**

The 106 Common Mistakes Homebuyers Make (and How to Avoid Them)

Chapter 1

Possibilities and Priorities

Mistake No. 1: **We thought about buying, but renting costs a lot less.**

Lesson: *Once you really compare all costs and benefits, you'll find renting costs far more than owning.*

In my STOP RENTING NOW!™ seminars, I nearly always meet renters who would like to own their own homes. But they hold back because they mistakenly believe that renting costs less than owning. In talking to hundreds of people who believe this, I've found three things they typically overlook: tax deductions, freedom, and long-term savings.

DON'T OVERLOOK YOUR TAX DEDUCTIONS

First, they forget about the tax deductions homeowners receive. Because mortgage interest and property taxes can be taken off your income taxes, your actual out-of-pocket home costs will run—depending on your combined federal, state, and local income tax rates—25 to 40 percent less than the check you write each month to your mortgage lender.

Let's say your house payment (principal, interest, property taxes, and insurance) will run $1,000 a month. Chances are, after considering the tax benefits of owning, that $1,000 will really only cost you about $700. An $1,800-a-month mortgage payment will probably cost you less than $1,200 a month. Or looked at in terms of rent, for example, if you're paying your landlord $500 a month, you could easily afford $750 to $800 a month for your own home.

Don't simply assume that owning costs more than renting. Talk to a Realtor or your tax advisor. Run through some specific figures for your area. Quite likely, you'll discover owning costs no more than renting—and frequently much less.

ESCAPE FROM RENTER'S JAIL

After buying her own home, Yolanda Jones told me, "I can't believe it. Not only am I saving money each month and building equity, but I feel like I've escaped from renter's jail." When I asked her what she meant by "renter's jail," Yolanda explained, "For the first time in my life I feel free. No more landlords to tell me how I can decorate, who I can have over, or whether I can get a dog. This is my home now, I'm free to do with it what I want. Even if it costs me more it'd be worth it."

Yolanda brings out a second point many renters overlook. When you own, you're not just buying a home, you're gaining freedom. As she says, you're escaping from renter's jail. If you're like Yolanda, the benefits of owning will far surpass the benefits of renting. So when figuring your rent vs. own cost comparisons, don't leave the enhanced benefits of owning out of your equation.

THINK LONG TERM

We've all heard dozens of times how America's corporate management has failed by focusing on the short term instead of the long term. Renters often make a similar mistake. In some high-cost areas of the country, even after allowing for tax benefits, the monthly costs of owning still may look higher than renting. If that's the situation in your area, you'll need to think long term. In fact, no matter where you live, the most important reason to buy a home is *not* to save money today. It's to save hundreds of thousands of dollars over the rest of your life.

Let's take an extreme case. Say you're paying $1,000 a month to rent. To buy (even after allowing for tax deductions) will cost you $1,500 a month. It sure looks like renting is cheaper. But this is a trap you don't want to fall into, because if you've got a fixed-rate mortgage, your costs of owning won't go up—and if at some later date you can refinance at lower interest rates, your monthly payments for owning will actually go down.

On the other hand, over the longer term, rents can only be expected to increase. Over time, your rents will catch up with your mortgage payments. After that—even at relatively modest rates of inflation, rent levels will be heading off to the stratosphere. Table 1.1 provides several examples of how rents will increase at rates of 4, 6, and 8 percent a year.

Some of the numbers in this table look impossibly large. But think about rent levels of the 1940s and 1950s. In most parts of the country, you could rent a house for $25 to $75 a month. Average house payments were $40 to $60 a month. Today's rent and mortgage payments often run 15 to 20 times higher than the amounts of those earlier years. Similarly, you can safely bet that when remembering back 20 or 30 years, people in the future will be talking about the ridiculously *low* rents of the 1990s. In contrast, today's homebuyers will still be enjoying mortgage payments at those "ridiculously" low 1990s prices well into the 21st century. Those who didn't buy will be paying (if they can afford them) rents three to ten times higher. And if we get another round of double-digit inflation similar to the one that occurred in the late 1970s and early 1980s, rents could be much higher than even the

Future Rents with Annual Increases of 4%			
		Years	
Monthly Rent	10	20	30	40
$500	$ 740	$1,095	$1,620	$2,400
$750	$1,100	$1,642	$2,430	$3,600
$1000	$1,420	$2,190	$3,240	$4,800

Future Rents with Annual Increases of 6%			
		Years	
Monthly Rent	10	20	30	40
$500	$ 895	$1,600	$2,850	$5,140
$750	$1,342	$2,400	$4,275	$7,710
$1000	$1,790	$3,200	$5,700	$10,280

Future Rents with Annual Increases of 8%			
		Years	
Monthly Rent	10	20	30	40
$500	$1,075	$2,330	$5,000	$10,850
$750	$1,612	$3,495	$7,500	$16,275
$1000	$2,150	$4,666	$10,000	$21,700

Table 1.1   Increasing Rents

figures in this table. Over time, owning costs far less than renting—and the benefits are far greater.

Mistake No. 2:   We would like to buy but we don't have enough savings for a down payment.

Lesson: *You don't need much savings for a down payment. You may not even need a down payment.*

I was listening to a talk-radio show recently. The subject being discussed was "no-money-down" home financing. Just as I tuned in I heard a caller angrily say, "I've been selling real estate for 25 years, and I've never seen a nothing-down deal." This real estate agent went on to complain about the "hucksters" pushing nothing-down seminars, books, and tapes who had gotten rich deceiving the public. "People who attend these seminars and watch too much late-night television just waste my time," this sales agent said. "I tell 'em when they call me, 'If you don't have the money to buy, go bother someone else.'"

Now contrast this agent's attitude with that of Realtor Joan Evans. "Anytime someone comes into our office seeking a rental," Joan says, "the first thing I do is ask them, 'Do you really want to rent? Or would you rather own?' More often than not, they say, 'Sure we would like to own but we don't have enough for a down payment.' When I hear that, that's when I go to work," Joan says. "One of the best parts of my job is to take renters who don't think they have enough money to buy and then figure out ways to turn them into homeowners. Granted, it's not a piece of cake; sometimes it takes six months or more. But I've found many of these buyers become my most loyal clients and a great source of referrals and repeat business."

If you are cash short, look for a Realtor like Joan Evans. Stay away from run-of-the-mill agents who show a don't-bother-me attitude to anyone with less than a five figure bank account. Here are some of the ways you can buy with little or no cash of your own.

- Borrow against (or withdraw) retirement funds
- Co-ownership
- Community reinvestment programs
- Contract-for-deed

- Department of Veterans Affairs (VA)
- Employer assistance
- Farmers Home Administration (FmHA)
- Federal Housing Administration (FHA)
- First-time buyer programs
- Fixer-uppers
- Gifts or loans from relatives or friends
- Lease-option
- Mortgage assumptions
- Not-for-profit housing developments
- Private mortgage insurance
- Real Estate Owned by mortgage lenders (REOs), foreclosures
- Sell other assets (car, boat, antiques, electronics)
- Seller financing
- Shared equity
- Special finance plans of new home builders
- State or local government down payment assistance programs
- Sweat equity

To discover how to buy cash short in your area, read closely the real estate sections and real estate ads of your local newspapers. Over the course of a month or two, you're likely to see many properties or finance plans that can be bought with little (or no) money down. Also, if you don't know an agent like Joan Evans, the real estate ads can help you turn up the names of Realtors who are willing to work with cash-poor home buyers.

Buying when you're cash poor may not prove easy. But a real estate professional who knows all the home-buying possibilities will be able to help you develop the financial planning and techniques you need to become a homeowner.

Mistake No. 3:   We can't afford to buy; the monthly payments are too high.

Lesson: If you can afford to rent, you can afford to own.

Before you convince yourself you can't afford to buy, make sure you compare your rent and mortgage payments on an *after-tax* basis. (See Mistake No. 1.) But if monthly payments still look too high, don't give up. There are many ways to get over the "unaffordable" monthly payment hurdle. Here's how Doreen Bierbrier did it.

At the time she bought her first home, Doreen says, "I was earning a modest salary (by Washington, D.C., standards) as a government worker. . . . The only way I could buy a house in a good neighborhood was to find one large enough to accommodate a couple of housemates who paid rent. If everything worked out, the rental income would cover more than half my house payment and two-thirds of the utilities. Adding in tax advantages and appreciation, I figured I would actually make money. Further, when the loan on the house was paid off, I would own a valuable asset free and clear."

As time has proven, Doreen had the right idea. While many moderately paid singles and couples have mistakenly pleaded "not enough income" to buy, others like Doreen have acted creatively and figured out ways to bridge the gap between their current earnings and affordability. In addition to taking in housemates, you might:

- Create an accessory apartment (sometimes called a mother-in-law suite) in your home by converting a garage, attic, or den.
- Reduce your monthly payments with an adjustable-rate mortgage.
- Reduce your monthly payments with a graduated-payment mortgage.
- Reduce your monthly payments by using a balloon mortgage.
- Bring in a co-owner.
- Buy a duplex, triplex, or other type of home that's already producing income that will help cover the monthly mortgage payments.
- See if you can locate a mortgage credit certificate (MCC) program in your area. Through MCCs, the federal government gives you a mortgage "subsidy" of $2,000 to $3,000 a year.
- Get a part-time job.
- Ask your employer for a raise or housing assistance.
- Reorganize your spending. Cut back on everything that ranks lower than home ownership on your scale of priorities.
- Reduce your debts. Sell off that extra car, boat, or furniture. Lock your credit cards in a drawer. Better yet, cut them in half.

At first glance—especially if you live in a high-cost area—it's sometimes easy to conclude that you can't afford the monthly payments on the home you want. But first make sure you consider the tax benefits of owning. Then start looking for creative ways to increase your income, cut your expenses, or use some type of affordable home finance plan. The successful home-buying experiences of millions of low- to moderate-income renters prove that if you can afford to rent, you can afford to buy.

Mistake No. 4:   No bank will give us a mortgage.

Lesson: *Many banks and mortgage lenders have special programs for hard-to-finance buyers. Even better, you may not even need bank financing.*

When Mary and Joe Cortez filed bankruptcy 18 months ago, they thought they had lost their chance to become homeowners. They were wrong. Just a little more than a year later, this couple successfully bought their first home with a low-down-payment FHA (Federal Housing Administration) loan. "We couldn't believe it," says Mary. "Our friends told us we wouldn't be able to get decent credit for years."

There's no doubt most mortgage lenders are a lot tougher to deal with these days. Since the widespread failures of hundreds of banks and savings and loans, credit standards have gotten tighter. But the good news is that mortgage lenders still need to make loans. And with thousands of potential mortgage lenders, if you're willing and able to make your mortgage payments on time, you can probably find the loan you need to buy a home.

As long as your credit problems are in the past (not the present), many lenders will give you a chance. This doesn't mean they're necessarily going to give you a mortgage. But if your problems were outside your control, or if you can convince the lender you've mended your spendthrift ways, many lenders will listen with a sympathetic ear. Even Fannie Mae (the Federal National Mortgage Corporation), which has about the tightest loan standards of any provider of mortgage funds, will sometimes accept a mortgage from former bankrupts within two years (or less) of their final discharge date.

Of course, more than likely you haven't filed bankruptcy or faced other serious credit problems. Nevertheless, many renters mistakenly believe that other kinds of problems will block them from getting a loan. Maybe you're self-employed or have been in your current job less than two years. Maybe you're a college student who works only part time. Maybe you want to spend 50 percent of your income for a home. Whatever your particular situation, don't simply assume you can't qualify. Ask around. Talk to knowledgable Realtors, mortgage brokers, or even other homebuyers who have faced the same kinds of problems you're facing.

I first started buying houses and small apartment buildings when I was an undergraduate college student. I had no established credit record, very small savings, and only a part-time job as a lab assistant. My strategy was to find older people who were tired of managing their rental properties, but liked the monthly income the properties gave them. These types of sellers proved to be great candidates for owner financing.

By selling their properties to someone who was young and ambitious, they got rid of the hassles of wayward tenants, stopped-up toilets, and furnace breakdowns in January. At the same time, the money they earned in interest on their seller mortgages gave them much better returns than they could have earned from bank savings accounts or certificates of deposit.

The great thing about owner financing is that owners are pretty much free to "lend" to whomever they please on whatever terms seem mutually beneficial.

So, if it turns out you really can't get a bank or savings institution to lend you the money you need to buy a home, look for owner-will-carry (OWC) financing. Or just skip the banks altogether. Many homebuyers and real estate investors don't even worry about qualifying for a mortgage with a typical lender. They simply prefer to finance their properties with their sellers.

Mistake No. 5:   Our agent told us to get prequalified by a lender so we would know exactly how much home we could afford.

Lesson: No lender can tell you exactly *how much home you can afford. Affordability depends on you, not just the lender.*

All across the country mortgage lenders and real estate agents are telling homebuyers to "get prequalified so you know exactly how much home you can afford." It's as if getting prequalified for a mortgage is like being measured for a custom-made suit. It isn't. How much home you can afford depends on you.

Can you increase your income? Can you cut your expenses? What type of home finance plan are you willing to use? Are MCC programs available in your area? Are first-time buyer programs available? What kinds of special financing incentives are new home builders or condo and townhouse developers offering? Do you have friends, relatives, or an employer who can make you a gift or a loan? Are you willing to buy a property that includes an accessory apartment or additional rental unit? How much are you willing to stretch your budget? Would you share your home with housemates? Can you buy jointly with someone else? Can you locate an owner who is willing to carry back financing? Are nonqualifying mortgage assumptions (FHA, Veterans Administration [VA]) available in your area?

How much home you can afford depends on answers to these and many other similar questions. When you start looking for a house, find a Realtor or mortgage lender who is skilled in *possibility* analysis. Don't rely on simple fill-in-the-blank prequalifying calculations or "instant" prequalifying computer programs. You have dozens (even hundreds) of ways to buy and finance your home. Thousands of mortgage lenders and thousands of property owners stand ready to make financing available.

Prequalifying with a specific lender can give you a general idea about how much you can spend based on your current finances and that lender's qualifying standards and loan programs. But it can't tell you all of your possibilities. Only through your own efforts of financial planning and possibility analysis can you really decide how much home you want and are able to afford.

Mistake No. 6:   Our agent said not to waste time looking at homes outside our price range.

Lesson: *You should learn as much as you can about homes priced above and below your "price range."*

This mistake follows from the "custom-made" suit type of prequalifying that's become so popular. Just as no one can tell you exactly "how much home you can afford," neither do you have a tightly defined "price range." Your price range depends on your possibility analysis. But there's another reason you should look at homes above and below your "price range." You can't know exactly what kind of home and neighborhood you want to aim for until you learn as much about the market as you can. Consider the experience of Sue and Bill Henderson.

Sue and Bill followed their agent's advice and looked only at homes in their "price range" of $90,000 to $100,000. Then after they bought, they were out driving around on a Sunday afternoon and went through some open houses in the $125,000 range.

"Wow," said Sue. "We had no idea $125,000 would buy so much more house than we got for our $97,500. These homes are bigger and a lot nicer. If we had known we would have stretched our budget and revamped our finances. Maybe we would have switched to an ARM [adjustable-rate mortgage] instead of using a fixed-rate mortgage. We could have even gotten a better school district."

Don't let someone pigeonhole you into a narrow price range. Look at a wide selection of homes and neighborhoods. Too many real estate agents will simply ask you, "How much would you like to spend (invest) in a home?" Now imagine walking into a new restaurant and sitting down at a table. The waiter comes up and asks, "What would you like to order?" You would probably say, "I don't know. We haven't seen the menu." Of course, you might also want to know what credit cards the restaurant accepts.

The situation's similar when shopping for a home. Make sure you've thoroughly looked over what's on the menu and what kinds of financing are available. And if you don't see what you want, maybe you should switch to a different neighborhood (just as you might look for another restaurant if you weren't satisfied with the menu or terms of credit). You might find you are willing to pay more than you first thought. Or you might decide to spend less. Maybe the $75,000 to $85,000 price range really gives you what you most need for now. Instead of spending $100,000, you can use the money you save for a more comfortable lifestyle, or perhaps other investments.

Whichever you choose, just don't fix on a home, neighborhood, and price range until you've looked at all kinds of properties and neighborhoods (within reason, of course). Learn all your options. With full knowledge of your choices and trade-offs, you'll make a better home-buying decision—a decision you'll be happy to live with.

Mistake No. 7: **Sure, we would like to buy our own home someday.**

Lesson: *Dreams move on if you wait too long. Put a plan into action now.*

Home buying requires a specific financial plan with specific dates and goals. In my STOP RENTING NOW!™ seminars, I frequently meet renters in their mid- to late 30s and early 40s who have yet to buy their first home. "Why didn't you buy earlier?" I ask them. "Well, we didn't think we could afford it," they often reply.

But this answer doesn't quite ring true. Why? Because from 20 years of teaching and working in real estate, I know that nearly everyone who wants to buy a home can buy a home—if they put their minds to it. So I probe further. "What do you mean when you say you couldn't afford to buy? How many mortgage lenders or knowledgeable real estate professionals did you talk to? How many owner-will-carry sellers did you contact? How many books and articles on home buying did you study? How closely and how frequently did you read the real estate and home builder ads in your local newspaper?" By asking them questions, I'm not trying to put them on the spot or make them feel bad. Rather, I want them to recognize the real reason they didn't buy wasn't "unaffordability." It was because they failed to set home buying as a primary goal.

They never educated themselves, planned their finances, or established a time frame to buy. Instead, they procrastinated. Although they knew they wanted to buy, it was always easier to put it off. As long as they told themselves they would buy *someday*, they avoided making the effort and doing the planning that home buying requires.

Unfortunately, procrastination and limp excuses have cost them tens (sometimes hundreds) of thousands of dollars. Try not to make this same mistake. Learn the lesson of the past. Don't wait for *someday*. Put a home-buying plan into action now. Set up a regular savings routine. Guard your credit record zealously. Don't spend (or borrow) money for things that are less important than owning your own home. Whether you want to buy this year, or maybe a year or two down the line, a plan now will make sure your goals (not dreams) come true.

Mistake No. 8: I wanted to wait until I got married.

Lesson: Don't postpone your plan to buy for some indefinite future.

In 1985 Megin Silver finished her MBA at the University of Virginia and took a good job in Washington, D.C. With one foot in the future, Megin eagerly accepted the challenge of work and career. But with one foot in the past, Megin was uncertain whether a single woman should embark on home ownership. "Anyway," Megin told herself, "I'll probably be married within a few years. It will be better to wait to buy until then."

Eight years have passed. Megin is still single. No marriage plans sit on the horizon. Yet during the time she's lived in D.C., Megin has watched Washington home prices more than double. She now wishes she had bought earlier. With a refinance at 1993's low interest rates, her mortgage payments would have fallen way below the amount she is paying for rent. Plus, she regrets missing out on eight years of tax deductions (which in her tax bracket she could certainly use) and thousands of dollars of equity buildup.

Last year one of every seven homes sold in the United States was bought by a single person. More than half of these singles were women. Just because you're single is no reason to put off buying. And if you can't get the home you want on your own income, don't forget you might cover your affordability gap by taking in housemates, buying a property with rental units, or bringing in a cobuyer.

Of course, "waiting to get married" is just one type of waiting for an indefinite time in the future. Some married couples I've met have postponed buying until they have kids. But then having kids itself keeps getting pushed farther into their future. "Waiting until I got married" or "waiting until we have kids" sounds like a plan. But it isn't. As a practical matter, waiting often turns out to be just as indefinite as *someday*. Don't wait for someday.

Mistake No. 9:   We were told not to buy unless we planned to stay put for at least four or five years.

Lesson: *Don't put off buying because you may be moving within a few years. Instead, execute a short-term ownership strategy.*

With recent home appreciation rates slowing to a crawl in some areas of the country, conventional wisdom says, "Don't buy unless you plan to stay put for at least four or five years." On the surface this advice sounds reasonable. When you sell after just two or three years, pay a real estate commission and closing costs, and your home hasn't appreciated much, you could end up losing several thousand dollars.

But what happens if you don't buy? Each year you continue to rent you're losing thousands of dollars in tax deductions. (See Mistake No. 1.) As another disadvantage, home prices, mortgage interest rates, or both could jump up quickly just as they have done in the past. Over time, those increases could cost you tens of thousands of dollars. Although you may incur some risks when you buy, keep in mind that you face even greater risks by not buying.

If you think you might move within a few years, your best bet is to develop a short-term ownership strategy. In her excellent book, *Housewise*, Suzanne Brangham tells how she bought and lived in more than a dozen homes in just 15 years. Suzanne says, "There is no wrong time to buy real estate. Regardless of the market, regardless of interest rates, I've turned a profit on my homes through good times and bad for the past 15 years." To achieve her profits, Suzanne buys homes she can improve. With her talents for redecorating and remodeling, Suzanne adds thousands of dollars in value to the homes she buys.

Buying "fixer-uppers" isn't the only way to execute a short-term ownership strategy, though. Reed Povitch boasts, "I make my money when I buy, not when I sell." Reed's strategy is to ferret out bargains. Sometimes he finds highly motivated owners; sometimes he buys at probate or foreclosure sales; on other occasions he buys REOs (real estate owned) from mortgage lenders who have taken back properties from borrowers who haven't made their payments.

To Robert Bruss, the highly respected nationally syndicated real estate columnist, the best short-term buying strategy is the lease-option. "By renting with an option to buy," Bruss advises, "you can establish your credit, build up cash (usually through rent credits) to use as a down payment, and you'll be protected against renewed inflation in housing prices."

A lease-option also gives you another benefit that's often over-looked. If during the option period home prices go up but you choose not to buy, you can sell the option for a profit to someone else. Then that person would be able to take advantage of your lower-than-market price and any rent credits you've earned.

In today's mobile society, many of us don't know where we're going to be living four or five years from now. Yet this uncertainty may continue for many years. To delay buying because you might move is generally a mistake. As a rule, you're better off to meet uncertainty with a short-term ownership strategy. (Remember, too, that even if you do move in a down market, you don't have to sell. Rent out the home and keep it as an investment until the market heats up again.)

Mistake No. 10:   We know exactly what we want.

Lesson: *Maybe. But more than likely you will change your mind. Plus, prepare yourself for trade-offs, compromises, and creativity.*

To be successful in buying a home that meets most of your wants and requirements, keep an open mind. Don't commit too early to a specific type of house, price range, or neighborhood. Until you really know the market, don't arbitrarily strike various houses and areas off your list of possibilities. Give them a fair chance to prove themselves.

Keeping an open mind is especially important when working with a real estate agent. Before a real estate professional begins to show you homes, he or she should sit down with you, get to know your feelings, and try to understand your concerns, likes, dislikes, and finances. The best real estate agents don't sell real estate. They solve problems.

Likewise, when you go to a doctor, you don't walk into his office and tell him what kind of prescription to write or describe in detail the kind of operation you think you need. Instead, a doctor asks you a battery of questions and takes some tests. Only after he or she gets to know you are potential remedies discussed.

First and foremost, both doctors and real estate agents should practice careful listening and "examination." As professionals knowledgeable in their fields, they may be able to suggest solutions you would have overlooked. That's what they're being paid for.

On the other hand, among the less successful agents in real estate, there's an old saying "Buyers are liars." This saying came about because the poorer agents see themselves as order takers and chauffeurs, not problem solvers. When first meeting someone who is thinking about buying a home, these agents will ask, "What are you looking for?" or "What price range do you have in mind?"

The buyers might answer, "Well, we'd like a three-bedroom, two-bath ranch, probably in Whitehall or River Ridge." Skipping the preliminaries, this type of agent "takes their order" and starts showing the couple houses. But as likely as not, the buyers don't buy from that agent. They end up with someone else. Then several weeks later the first agent learns the buyers just had their offer accepted on a duplex in Hyde Park. Over coffee at the nearby Dunkin Donuts, the agent mutters, "Well, it's happened again. Those folks were just wasting my time. It just proves 'buyers *are* liars.'"

Of course, the couple wasn't lying to the agent. They said they wanted a three-bedroom in Whitehall because that's what they thought they wanted. They really hadn't explored their options. After they began to consider the relative advantages and disadvantages of various properties, they changed their minds.

Chances are you won't buy the type of house you now have in mind. It may not exist. It may cost too much. You might discover other homes you like better. You might decide to trade off some features (property or neighborhood) for other features (fix-up value or investment potential) that you previously hadn't paid much attention to. Maybe through creativity you will figure out a way to overcome the objections to a property (or neighborhood) you originally thought were critical. Or maybe, after all is said and done, you really will find the exact home you know you want. Just don't close your mind too soon to other possibilities.

And make sure the agent you work with wants to do more than take your order and chauffeur you around. Get an agent who thinks creatively and knows how to solve problems. At least at first, a good agent will spend more time listening than talking. Before an agent can know what you want, he or she must get to know you.

Mistake No. 11:   We have to have a pool.

WANTS   _NEEDS_

Lesson: *Don't let the tail wag the dog.*

When Carol and Blair Alsop moved from Michigan to Florida, they decided their new home must have a swimming pool. This was the first priority on their list of features. "We only want to look at homes with pools," the Alsops told their Realtor. Even when their Realtor tried to get the couple to consider other homes that would meet most of their other requirements, they refused. "Nope, we got to have a pool," they emphasized.

As it turned out, though, none of the pool homes they could find really hit their hot spots. The homes were either too large or too small. They needed repairs. They were located in the wrong neighborhoods or school districts. Sometimes they cost too much. Nothing they saw really seemed to click. Finally their Realtor was able to persuade the couple to at least look at a home that had just come on the market.

Except for the swimming pool, the home had everything the Alsops could hope for. It was the right size; the right neighborhood; and, best of all, the right price. The sellers were even willing to carry back financing at a point less than current bank mortgage rates. The Alsops were tempted. But they said no. "If we're going to live in Florida, we're going to have a pool."

Eventually the Alsops did buy a home. They paid more than they really wanted. The home needed repairs. It was larger than they needed. And the location wasn't their first choice. But it did have a pool.

Unfortunately, shortly after moving into their new home, the Alsops knew they had made a mistake. They didn't use the pool as much as they thought they would. The pool and the house cost too much for maintenance and repairs, and the commute to work was longer than they liked. Within two years after they had bought, they sold the house and moved. Their new house didn't have a pool.

Now don't misunderstand. By recounting this experience, I'm not talking against buying a home with a swimming pool. The Alsops' mistake was not in buying a home with a pool. Their mistake was insisting that one feature of their home should outweigh the importance of all other features. The Alsops really weren't being true to themselves. They had fixated on an idealized image of Florida living—and to their mind that type of living included poolside parties, after-work swims for exercise and relaxation, and Saturday morning brunch on the patio.

All these things sounded great. But the necessities of career ambitions, running a household, and raising a family put considerable distance between their imagined lifestyle and the reality of their everyday living.

When you shop for a house, put first things first. Don't insist on a pool, a third or fourth bedroom, a formal dining room, a formal living room, a den, a fireplace, a two-car garage, a big yard, colonial architecture, a view, or any other features that are not critical to the primary benefits your home and neighborhood must provide. Be willing to trade off an idealized image for the way you will actually live.

We all have certain features that we would like in our dream homes. Yet it's usually a mistake to let these "dream" features override our better judgment. Try to clearly distinguish your wants from your needs. In other words, don't let the tail wag the dog.

Mistake No. 12:   We liked the house on Elmwood best, but our furniture wouldn't work there.

Lesson: *Buy furniture to fit your new house. Don't buy a new house to fit your old furniture.*

Real estate agents frequently say they can tell when many buyers get really interested in a house. The tape measure is pulled out and the prospective buyers try to figure out whether their furniture will fit in the home. In somewhat similar fashion, some people will flat out reject a house because "there's no way our furniture will work there." Clearly this is putting the cart before the horse. Your needs should govern your choice of a home, not previous decisions you've made about your furniture.

In fact, I confess that I almost made this mistake several years ago. At the time, I owned a 3,000-square-foot house and was planning a move to a new area. Upon learning I was single, the agent I was working with suggested several homes she thought I would like in the 1,800- to 2,000-square-foot range. "Oh, my," I said, "those are much too small. I could never get my furniture to fit in those houses."

Then I began to recall how I had come to acquire a 3,000-square-foot house. I didn't really want or need such a large home. I had bought it because the house had great views of a lake and was located in a very private setting. Naturally, after I bought the house, I filled it with furniture.

So here I was just about ready to reject smaller (and more sensible) homes because my furniture wouldn't fit. Fortunately, after thinking through the ridiculousness of the situation, I sold some furniture and bought a 1,700-square-foot house that I enjoyed much more than I had the larger home.

Like many other people, I had almost let past decisions set the course for my future decisions. We really are creatures of habit. But a major decision like buying a home should prompt us to reevaluate old habits and old decisions. Whether it's your furniture or some other previous decision, try to distinguish the way you have lived in the past from how you would most like to live in the future. Don't unconsciously let your past become prologue.

Mistake No. 13:   There were so many rules it was like living under socialism.

Lesson: *When going over your objectives and priorities, don't just think of home features and neighborhoods. Also consider the types of homeowner association rules and regulations you want to live under.*

If you buy into a co-op, condo, townhouse, or recently built (less than 20 years old) subdivision development, more than likely you're going to be governed by a homeowners association. Although a homeowners association can't put you in jail, it can require you to live under its rules and regulations; fine you for violations; put a lien against your home if you don't pay your fines, assessments, or monthly dues; and otherwise make your life unpleasant.

After Chuck and Michelle Kane bought their new home, one of the first things they wanted to do was to put in a yard. So Chuck took the first weekend and planted grass seed. Two days later a representative of the homeowners association stopped by to tell Chuck the bad news. In that subdivision, grass seed was not permitted. To comply with association regulations, the Kanes would have to sod their yard. And just as a reminder to encourage the Kanes to follow all other homeowners association rules, the association fined the Kanes $400.

Once Chuck and Michelle really started to look over the rules they would have to live under, they learned:

- Their homeowners association would have to approve any exterior design changes or painting they planned for their home.
- Chuck couldn't park his antique Chevy in his driveway while he worked on it.
- The Kanes couldn't put a Sears storage shed in their backyard.
- No outside clotheslines or television antenna or satellite dishes were permitted.

When Anita Maertz bought her townhouse, she knew civil rights laws forced the townhouse development to accept her sons, age four and six. Except for certain housing developments for seniors, neither rental companies nor homeowner associations may exclude children. But accepting children because of the law and making them welcome are two different issues.

After Anita moved in, she discovered that kids could not play on the grounds of the development. Parents were supposed to take them to a nearby park. "Sure, we accept kids here," Anita remembers one disgruntled resident telling her. Then he added, "We just don't tolerate them."

To make her new home livable, Anita joined the board of the association, formed a political coalition with other parents, and eventually got the rules changed to try to create a "children-friendly" environment. "It was a lot of time and effort," Anita recalled. "But we had no choice. It's our home too and our kids should have the right to play here."

Of course, from her viewpoint Anita is right. But others without children may also feel they have a right to peace and quiet. Unfortunately, there's no easy answer to the question "What rules and regulations should the association promulgate and enforce?" How would you judge rules such as these?

- No more than one pet is allowed per unit. Maximum weight of a pet shall not exceed 15 pounds.
- A pet deemed by the Board to be noisy or uncontrollable must be disposed of within three days notice.
- No automobile mechanical work whatsoever will be permitted on the premises.
- Bicycles must be stored in designated areas. They must not be left on the grounds, in hallways, or stored on patios or balconies.

- Personal conduct and attire in the common areas are subject to approval of the Board.
- No signs ("for sale" or "for rent") shall be displayed in any manner whatsoever.
- No owner/occupant shall install drapes or curtains within any unit unless such drapes have a white liner visible from outside the unit.
- No entertaining of more than 10 persons within a given unit shall be permitted.
- Any owner who wants to offer his or her unit for rent must first obtain the approval of the Board. All tenants also must be approved by the Board.
- No leases beyond a duration of one year are permitted.
- The Board retains the right to disapprove a new purchaser in the development for any lawful reason it deems appropriate.
- No driveway basketball hoops and playing areas are permitted.
- No treehouses may be built.

Homeowners association rules and regulations can touch upon nearly anything you might want to do. So before you choose a development for consideration, closely review the "laws" you will have to live under. Since homeowners associations and boards are supposed to be run democratically, most rules and regulations operate to enhance the value and livability of the development. For some homeowners, though, democratic rule means "tyranny by the majority." The rules imposed are just too "socialistic."

Mistake No. 14: What! Beans for dinner again?

Lesson: Put as much money as you can into your home. But don't underestimate your other necessary living expenses.

Most financial advisors recommend that at least for your first home, you should stretch your budget as far as possible to buy as much home as you can. Generally, this advice is sound. The logic is that as your income goes up over time, your fixed mortgage payments will take a smaller and smaller percentage of your income. Although things might be tight for a few years, as long as your career is on an upward path, you'll soon move into your comfort zone.

What is true generally, however, may not be true specifically. Before you stretch too far to buy, prepare a very realistic (even pessimistic, perhaps) postpurchase budget. If you're borrowing part of your down payment or planning to spend money improving your house, make sure you allow for those additional payments. If you are using an adjustable-rate mortgage, figure out how well you could manage financially over the coming years if the interest rate on your ARM moves up each year to its maximum rate.

Especially after you've been looking for a home over a number of months, it's sometimes easy to convince yourself that you should increase your price range. Or maybe you find the perfect house, but it's $40,000 more than you had in mind. You start thinking, "Well, we can borrow $10,000 from Mom and Dad. We can put next summer's vacation on the Visa card. Plus, we both will probably be getting raises next year. And even though this house means a longer commute, the extra gas won't cost that much." When thoughts like these start running through your mind, you're not really making budget decisions. You're simply rationalizing.

Still, maybe you should stretch to buy. Before you commit, though, write the figures down and (as we would say in business school) run through various financial scenarios. If you really feel satisfied with what you see, go for it. If looking at the numbers makes you feel a bit queasy, ask yourself whether you really would be happy on a steady diet of rice, spaghetti, or beans. Everyone *should* own a home. No one should let a home own them.

Mistake No. 15:   We bought because we got so tired of looking.

Lesson: Never buy just to "get the decision over with."

Home buying presents a paradox. Planning to buy can give you one of the most exciting times of your life. Most everyone enjoys getting up early Sunday morning, bringing in the newspaper, poring over the homes for sale, and then later going out and touring neighborhoods looking at open houses, exploring possibilities, and imagining what life will be like in a new home. But searching for the *right* home can also frustrate and depress. At some point, you may reach the let's-forget-the-whole-thing stage. Or frequently even worse, you may make a let's-just-buy-something-and-get-it-over-with type of choice.

If you do begin to feel confused, uncertain, and frustrated, don't let these feelings influence your decision. Instead, back up and ask yourself these questions:

- Have we lost touch with our most important feelings, needs, priorities, and goals?
- Do we want to have it all? Are we looking for the perfect home?
- Do we lack confidence in our ability to make a good decision?
- Do our wants or goals lie outside market realities or our financial means?
- Are we buying for ourselves? Or are we worrying about how our friends, relatives, or parents will judge our decision?
- Have we really explored a full range of options and possibilities?
- Have we developed a sensible time schedule for getting to know the market and finding a home?
- Is our ability to choose being unduly influenced by an idealized self-image?
- Can we recast problems as opportunities?

By asking these questions, you can probably pinpoint the reasons you're feeling confused, uncertain, or frustrated. More than likely you're being tugged in different directions because you haven't explicitly identified all the various emotions pushing and pulling you first one way and then another. Decision-making expert, Dr. Theodore Rubin, calls this type of indecisiveness the chairman-is-missing syndrome. By thinking truthfully (remember, we all try to deceive ourselves) about the issues raised by these questions, you can reestablish control over your decision-making. You'll pound your gavel. Your inner "chairman" can then bring your internal confusion to order.

Mistake No. 16: Why didn't we think of that before?

Lesson: *Once you've made a decision, don't agonize over what "you woulda, coulda, or shoulda" done. Commit to the decision you've made.*

All too often, home buyers begin to feel "buyer's remorse." They start worrying about all the things they didn't think of or the things they should have done. Don't make this mistake. You'll be wasting energy and emotion. If you've put your "chairman" in control of your home-buying efforts, you'll make a good decision.

Once you've made your choice, don't look back. Plan for your future. Concentrate on how you can make your decision work. "The failure of a decision," says Dr. Rubin, "has little or nothing to do with the choice." When "failure" does occur, it's nearly always "directly traceable and proportional to lack of dedicated commitment."

Success occurs when you decide to buy. From then on, happiness in your new home will depend on your loyalty and commitment to that choice. With the right attitude and planning, you will make your choice a good choice.

Chapter 2

Your Home as an Investment

Mistake No. 17: **We're not planning to buy. Many of the experts say home prices won't appreciate in the future as they have in the past.**

Lesson: *Experts have been predicting "home prices have reached their peak" for the past 50 years.*

From the late 1980s through the early 1990s, the media has found dozens of experts who have warned homebuyers not to consider their homes as investments. "Buy a home as a comfortable place to live," they say. "But don't expect much appreciation. The days of sure-fire price increases are over."

Among all the lessons history teaches, none is more certain than (in general) home prices go up. Regardless how high you think prices are today, they will be higher 10 years from now. And much, much higher 20 or 30 years into the future. Don't make the mistake of believing "home prices have reached their peak." Before you put faith in the naysaying of economic "experts," take a quick trip through their predictions of earlier years:

- The prices of houses seem to have reached a plateau and there is reasonable expectancy that prices will decline. (*Time*, December 1, 1947)

- Houses cost too much for the mass market. Today's average price is around $8,000—out of reach for two-thirds of all buyers. (*Science Digest*, April 1948)

- If you have bought your house since the War . . . you have made your deal at the top of the market. . . . The days when you couldn't lose on a house purchase are no longer with us. (*House Beautiful*, November 1948)

- The goal of owning a home seems to be getting beyond the reach of more and more Americans. The typical new house today costs about $28,000. (*Business Week*, September 4, 1969)

- You might well be suspicious of a "common wisdom" that tells you, "Don't wait, buy now. . . . Continuing inflation will force home prices and rents higher and higher." (*NEA Journal*, December 1970)

- The median price of a home today is approaching $50,000. . . . Housing experts predict price rises in the future won't be that great. (*Nations Business*, June 1977)

- The era of easy profits in real estate may be drawing to a close. (*Money*, January 1981)

- In California . . . for example, it is not unusual to find families of average means buying $100,000 houses. . . . I'm confident prices have passed their peak. (John Wesley English and Gray Emerson Cardiff, *The Coming Real Estate Crash*, 1980)

- If you're looking to buy, be careful. Rising home values are not a sure thing anymore. (*Miami Herald*, October 25, 1985)

- The golden-age of risk-free run-ups in home prices is gone. (*Money*, March 1985)

- Most economists agree . . . [a home] will become little more than a roof and a tax deduction, certainly not the lucrative investment it was through much of the 1980s. (*Money*, April 1986)

- We're starting to go back to the time when you bought a home not for its potential money-making abilities, but rather as a nesting spot. (*Los Angeles Times*, January 31, 1993)

- Financial planners agree that houses will continue to be a poor investment. (*Kiplinger's Personal Financial Magazine*, November 1993)

Don't confuse down periods in the real estate cycle with long-term price trends. Since World War II, home prices have frequently jumped by 10 or 20 percent a year. On occasion, they've held steady for as long as three to five years. And in cities that have experienced severe downturns in their local economies, prices have sometimes fallen temporarily. During the early 1970s, for example, large layoffs at Boeing drove Seattle home prices down by 20 to 30 percent. A local billboard went up with the request, "Will the last person to leave Seattle please turn out the lights?" Yet Seattle recovered. Now prices there are four times higher than they were in 1971.

Likewise, in the coming years, we will look back to the home prices of other more recently hard-hit cities such as Denver, Dallas, Houston, San Diego, Boston, and New York. We'll say, "Boy, those were the days. Can you believe I could have picked up a three-bedroom, two-bath home in Clairemont for just $225,000?" And no doubt, in the year 2001, we will hear the "experts" tell us, "Home prices can't go any higher. Just since the early 1990s the median price of a home has jumped from $110,000 to $190,000. The days are gone when like during the 1990s, buying a home for investment was a sure thing."

Mistake No. 18:   *The experts were wrong in the past, but things are different today.*

Lesson: *The more things change, the more they remain the same.*

Experts have always put forth plausible reasons to support their predictions that home prices had reached their peak. In 1947 housing economist John Dean wrote that large jumps in home prices in the 1940s had occurred because of "rapid population growth, inflation, and housing shortages." Then he added, "None of these is likely to continue."

In fact, though, what have we seen during the past 50 years? Recurring periods of rapid population growth, inflation, and housing shortages. And what about the future?

The most recent estimates of the U.S. Bureau of Census show that during the next 10 years, the U.S. population will grow by more than 20 million people. Increasing numbers of births (the echo boom), millions of immigrants, and longer life expectancies are adding record numbers to our population. To house these 20 million people will require around 8 million new homes and apartments. In addition, we'll need between 5 and 10 million homes to replace those that are lost because of fires, abandonment, conversion to commercial uses, and natural disasters (earthquakes, floods, hurricanes, tornadoes).

When (as they teach in Economics 101) we turn to the supply side of the equation, we'll find that the number of new homes being built falls far below the numbers that will be needed—especially in the low- to moderate-price ranges. During the recession of the early 1990s, fewer apartments were built than at any time since World War II. New home construction was also down substantially. It's almost certain that at some point within the next several years, we are going to experience tight housing markets again. As of early 1994, both apartment vacancy rates and inventories of unsold homes were falling.

Recent economic news regarding inflation has generally been good. "Inflation has been squeezed out of the economy," the headlines tell us. But has it really? Or are we deceiving ourselves? During the past five years, consumer prices have increased, on average, around 4 to 5 percent a year. This rate of inflation does seem low compared to the 10 to 13 percent rates we experienced in the early 1980s. Historically, though, an average annual inflation rate of 4 plus percent is not low.

Throughout the 1950s until the mid-1960s, inflation ranged between 1 and 2 percent a year. Even between the years 1966 to 1973, annual inflation averaged "only" 4.3 percent. No one at that time, however, thought inflation was low. Most economists were so alarmed about "runaway prices" that in 1973, Herbert Stein, President Nixon's chairman of the Council of Economic Advisors, persuaded the President to impose wage and price controls all across the United States.

Relative to the late 1970s and early 1980s, today's inflation rates are low. Relative to most of our postwar history, they are high. As Mark Twain might have observed were he still with us, "The death of inflation has been greatly exaggerated." With a growing population, a reduced supply of homes, and continued inflation, the same factors that have pushed up home prices in the past will again push them up in the future.

Mistake No. 19:   *Lower rates of inflation mean lower rates of appreciation for homes.*

Lesson: *Reduced rates of inflation can actually lead to higher rates of appreciation.*

Conventional wisdom holds that strong rates of appreciation in home prices depend on high rates of inflation. The logic of this argument seems straightforward. It goes like this: With rapidly rising prices for labor and materials, home builders cut back on their new construction and raise their prices. With higher prices for new homes, many homebuyers switch to the resale market and buy existing homes. With more buyers bidding for existing homes, these home prices are pushed up. Increasing demand and a reduced supply of new and existing homes for sale yield strong rates of appreciation for home values.

The only problem with this argument is that it contradicts the facts. Ask any Realtor or home builder who lived through the double-digit rates of inflation of the early 1980s. Contrary to today's recollections, those were not generally good times for real estate. Reporting on the Southern California market of 1982, a leading national newspaper wrote, "Not only are asking prices falling, but in some cases people who have bought homes in the last few years are selling them for less than they paid for them. . . . Now people are buying shelter. . . ." And recall the *Money* magazine article of January 1981. (See Mistake No. 17.) "The era of easy profits in real estate may be drawing to a close," *Money* told its readers.

Although over time higher rates of inflation will add to building costs, rapidly rising prices also cause interest rates to rise. As interest rates go up, home affordability goes down. People who might like to buy are blocked from the market. Sooner or later, demand for homes falls because with higher interest rates homebuyers can't qualify for financing. Fewer buyers bring price increases to a halt.

On the other hand, lower rates of inflation mean lower interest rates. With lower mortgage interest, more people can afford to buy. If predictions of lower inflation for the remainder of the 1990s are correct, millions of Americans who would be shut out of the mortgage market with interest rates at 10 to 14 percent—the rates that prevailed throughout most of the 1980s—will be able to own their own homes. More buyers will push prices higher.

In fact, if we look at the 1980s, it wasn't the high inflation years that brought the steepest home price increases. The greatest rates of appreciation (except for the oil belt, see Mistake No. 25) occurred between 1985 and 1988.

Then, in 1989, inflation climbed back up close to 5 percent. It was the largest increase in the Consumer Price Index (CPI) since 1982. Mortgage interest rates again went over 10 percent in 1989. Home prices stalled (and even retreated) in many cities where appreciation rates had been the strongest. Construction of new homes fell. Defense-related industries suffered cutbacks and layoffs. To become more competitive, large firms with bloated managerial bureaucracies, such as General Motors and IBM, shed employees. The country experienced its seventh post–World War II recession and slowdown in economic growth.

Now the country is firmly back on its path of rising incomes and employment. Mortgage affordability looks much better than it did during the 1980s. Large firms have dramatically improved their productivity. American steel, auto, and high-technology firms lead the world as low-cost producers of quality products.

Although it's true that higher rates of inflation lead to increased building costs and eventually higher home prices, lower rates of inflation can yield a stronger economy, more jobs, lower mortgage interest rates, and more homebuyers. Don't make the mistake of believing that a slower upward drift of the CPI means weak appreciation in home prices. Between 1950 and 1970 average home prices tripled $(10,000 to nearly $30,000). During this same 20 years, increases in the CPI averaged less than 3 percent a year.

Mistake No. 20:   *We thought we could make higher returns investing in stocks.*

Lesson: *Even with "low" rates of appreciation, most likely a home will still prove to be your best investment.*

Colin and Melinda Stein recently announced proudly to a reporter who was interviewing them, "We earn $80,000 a year and don't own a home. We could buy if we wanted to. But we thought we could do better investing in stocks. At best, we think homes will only appreciate 4 or 5 percent a year. We can make a lot higher returns in the market."

"Right now," says an article in *U.S. News & World Report* (April 10, 1991, p. 61), a couple who puts 10 percent down on a home priced at $94,200, "would have to own for eight years to come out ahead of where they would be if instead they had rented and invested in Treasury bonds, currently earning about 8 percent." This analysis, the article says, "assumes an average annual [home] appreciation rate of 4 percent. Economists predict that may be the norm for the 1990s, a decade in which renters could turn out to be the smartest investors of all."

"Renters could turn out to be the smartest investors of all." That seems to be a consistent theme of many media articles, and unfortunately many potential homebuyers have accepted it without serious question. But do the numbers really support the conclusion? No.

To make the example simple, let's say a couple invests $10,000 in a $100,000 home. Assuming they financed their purchase with a 30-year, $90,000 mortgage at 7.75 percent, after eight years their outstanding mortgage balance would have been paid down to $81,585. With 4 percent a year appreciation for eight years, their home's value would have grown to $136,860. If we subtract the couple's mortgage balance ($81,585) from their home's value of $136,860, we find their original $10,000 investment has increased more than fivefold to $55,275 of homeowners' equity. That's the equivalent of an after-tax rate of return of around 24 percent a year.

If this couple were in a 30 percent marginal income tax bracket, their annual after-tax return on their 8 percent Treasury bond investment would equal just 5.6 percent. If the couple had bought stocks, they may have done better. But their returns would still have fallen well below the returns of home ownership—even at a 4 percent rate of home appreciation.

Depending on whose numbers you use, over the longer run stocks have yielded an average pretax return of between 9 and 12 percent a year. On an after-tax basis, a 10 percent-a-year return on stocks is considered very good. In fact, over the long term, fewer than two percent of professional fund managers have been able to consistently earn after-tax returns on stocks of more than 10 to 15 percent a year.

Consider, for example, that in 1965 the Dow Jones stock index stood at 910.88. By 1982 this index of blue chip companies actually stood slightly lower, at 884.36. During this entire 17-year period, the Dow Jones index went no higher than 974.92. And it fell to as low as 753.19 in 1970.

With home price increases slowing during the past several years—and with the stock market hitting record highs—we've lost our historical perspective. Stock markets and home prices run in cycles. Putting $10,000 into the stock market in 1989 could have yielded better returns by early 1994 than a $10,000 investment in a home in San Diego or Boston. (But certainly not in Seattle, Denver, Chicago, Miami, Austin, or Portland.)

Over longer periods of time, though, an investment in a home can be expected to outperform the stock market. With a home you get the magic benefits of leverage. You invest a relatively small down payment. You receive returns based on increases in the total value of your home. That's why even a "lowly" 4 percent annual rate of appreciation will nearly always outperform the returns you could get from stocks or bonds. And not only is home ownership far less risky than stocks or bonds, stocks and bonds won't keep you dry when it rains or warm when the weather is freezing cold.

Mistake No. 21:   *We weren't concerned about our home as an investment; we just wanted a comfortable place to live.*

Lesson: *When shopping for a home, you should always factor potential appreciation gains into your decision.*

With so much recent talk about "homes no longer being a 'sure-fire' investment," many homebuyers have scratched "investment" off their list of criteria to judge a home. This is a mistake. In both hot and cold markets, you should compare homes and neighborhoods on the basis of your profit potential. Don't adopt the attitude "Well, if it appreciates, great. If not, we still have gained all the benefits of living in our own home."

No matter how bleak your local housing market may appear, good opportunities for profit are always available to those who remain savvy and persistent in their home-buying efforts. Your overall market may not be making headlines with big jumps in prices. But that doesn't mean you can't "beat the market" if you want to.

Just before California headed into recession in 1989, Beth Rosander got divorced. With two children to raise and no job prospects, Beth decided to make a living buying rundown houses, fixing them up, and then quickly reselling them. If Beth had paid attention to the newspapers, she would have known the California "boom" in housing prices had stalled. No way could she expect to make money buying and selling homes. Couldn't she see? Homes were no longer a good investment.

Fortunately, Beth ignored the steady stream of bad news. Between the years 1988 and 1993, Beth bought, fixed up, and sold six houses. After each sale, she pocketed between $20,000 and $40,000. Remember, too, that Beth bought these houses without income from a job. Bank loans were out of the question. To solve this problem, Beth financed each of her purchases with the sellers of the homes. "The deals are not there with a big red flag," Beth points out. "I had to weed through [literally as well as figuratively, I suspect] a lot of properties and get up to speed on the market" (*San Francisco Examiner*, May 2, 1993, p. F-1).

Maybe buying a fixer-upper isn't your cup of tea. But that's not the only way to make your home a good investment even in down markets. You also can shop to buy at a bargain price. Make your money when you buy, not when you sell. And you can try to locate neighborhoods that appreciate faster than average. Nearly every city has "hot" neighborhoods or communities that show far more promise for gains than overall trends in prices would seem to indicate.

How do you locate these promising neighborhoods or communities? Here are eight indicators of emerging hot spots.

1. You can anticipate an upward trend in prices when the number of days it takes to sell a home in a given neighborhood is falling. If last year homes took an average of 120 days to sell, an average time on market this year of 45 days would normally signal price gains are just around the corner.

2. The gap between listing prices and selling prices is narrowing. Normally homes sell within 5 to 10 percent of their listing price. If average selling prices climb within less than 5 percent of their listing prices, sellers are likely to begin boosting their prices.

3. An increasing percentage of the homes are being sold to people moving into the neighborhood from another area of the city or from out of town. This figure shows the "hot" neighborhood or community is gaining in popularity vis-à-vis other areas.

4. The income, education, and occupation levels of the people moving into an area are generally higher than the neighborhood's current residents. (Note: Don't mistakenly assume that changing ethnicity of a neighborhood means property values will fall. Such stereotypical views belong to the 1950s. Irrespective of its ethnic makeup, in our times, experience shows any neighborhood can achieve substantial gains in desirability and value.)

5. New and existing homeowners in the neighborhood are investing in home remodeling and renovations. Home builders are constructing new homes in the area. Typically, increasing investment means increasing values.

6. The percentage of homes in the neighborhood occupied by owners (as opposed to renters) is increasing. Even viewed alone, this statistic is almost a 100 percent indicator of rising home values. It is

virtually certain that a neighborhood will appreciate strongly as homeowners displace renters and absentee landlords.

7. Transportation arteries are improving access to the area. Better roads, a new bridge, or extension of a mass transit facility can each push property values up dramatically. If your city has any major new (or improved) access routes or facilities planned, figure out which neighborhoods and communities stand to gain much faster commutes to major job centers.

8. The neighborhood has an active community or homeowners association that zealously works to protect and enhance living conditions in the area. These activities may involve anything from "Take Pride in Your Home" campaigns, to school improvement programs, to crime prevention measures. An active neighborhood association shows that people care about their homes and their property values.

Even in "down" markets, opportunities for home-buying profits always exist. Over time, the differences in profit potential among various homes and neighborhoods can mean tens of thousands of dollars to you. When you're choosing your home, don't overlook this potential. In the end, you may still decide to opt for just "a comfortable place to live." But make this trade-off—if you see it is a trade-off—consciously, not unconsciously.

Mistake No. 22:   *We were told to buy in the best neighborhood we could afford. The best neighborhoods always appreciate the fastest.*

Lesson: *Evaluate neighborhoods specifically for their investment potential. Never assume a "good" neighborhood will appreciate faster than an "inferior" one.*

In the past, few homebuyers have explicitly investigated and compared neighborhoods for their appreciation potential. Conventional wisdom told them "Buy in the best neighborhood you can afford. The best neighborhoods always appreciate fastest." Not true. As a "comfortable place to live," you might want to consider only the "better" neighborhoods, but don't necessarily assume these neighborhoods will appreciate faster than "less desirable" ones.

Between 1989 and 1993, the most expensive homes in Beverly Hills, California, fell in value by 20 to 30 percent. During this same period, homes in Watts and south-central Los Angeles *increased* in value by 30 percent.

Granted, this comparison is extreme. But the general principle holds: Look for the flashing green lights that signal a neighborhood or community is on the move. (See Mistake No. 21.) It's highly unlikely that one neighborhood can consistently appreciate faster than an alternative neighborhood for an indefinite period of time. Once you think about it, you can easily see why above-average appreciation rates can't last forever.

Say most homebuyers prefer Hidden Valley Estates over the Swampy River subdivision. Homes in Hidden Valley sell for an average price of $150,000. Homes in Swampy River go for about $100,000. Because buyers favor Hidden Valley, its homes have been appreciating at 8 percent a year. In contrast, appreciation in Swampy River has been limping along at just 2 percent a year. Yet can you count on this trend to continue? Maybe; maybe not.

With five more years of 8 percent appreciation, home prices in Hidden Valley Estates would climb from $150,000 to $220,000. Those Swampy River homes—at a yearly appreciation rate of 2 percent— would be worth $110,000. Hidden Valley homes now cost twice as much as homes in Swampy River. After another five years of similar appreciation, Hidden Valley homes would cost nearly $325,000. Swampy River home prices would come in at $121,000.

More than likely, at some point well before 10 years have passed, most would-be buyers are going to be priced out of Hidden Valley Estates. Instead, they'll meander through Swampy River. "Well, this place has possibilities," they might say. Before long, as homebuyers switch from Hidden Valley to Swampy River, Hidden Valley appreciation rates will begin to fall. Swampy River appreciation rates will begin to rise.

The new Swampy River homeowners will then join with other residents and change the name of the Swampy River subdivision to the River View Plantation. They'll start sprucing up their homes. They will organize a Neighborhood Watch program. And they will pass a bond measure to improve the local schools, libraries, and parks. Within a few short years, River View (a.k.a. Swampy River) will emerge as one of the fastest-appreciating neighborhoods in the area.

But it probably won't last. After five years (more or less), homes in River View may also become "overpriced" relative to other neighborhoods and subdivisions. Price increases there will settle down a bit. Appreciation rates in other areas will pick up speed. Savvy home buyers will create another "hot" neighborhood.

Price trends among types of homes, neighborhoods, and communities nearly always run in cycles. Don't assume past appreciation (slow or fast) points to more of the same. Investigate market signals. Compare the *relative* costs, benefits, and features of various homes and areas. "Inferior" neighborhoods often outperform their betters.

Mistake No. 23:   *We were told never to buy the biggest or most expensive house in the neighborhood.*

Lesson: *Buy the home that offers the best value as measured against your needs and objectives.*

You've probably heard the common advice, "Don't buy the biggest or most expensive house in the neighborhood." Supposedly, the surrounding smaller, lower-priced homes will bring down the value of the more expensive house. As a result, your home's appreciation rate won't be as good as the other homes in the neighborhood. Once you think about it, though, the advice fails to make sense.

Say the smaller homes in the neighborhood appreciate at 6 percent a year. The largest homes appreciate at 2 percent. With the passing of years, the smaller houses would come to sell for more than the larger houses—which, of course, is not likely. In other words, the rules of compound interest work to invalidate this simplistic advice, just as they also prove false the claims that "the best neighborhoods always appreciate the fastest." (See Mistake No. 23.) To illustrate:

Purchase Price	Home Values			
	2 Years	4 Years	6 Years	8 Years
$100,000 (6% apprec. for smaller homes)	$112,360	$126,250	$141,850	$159,380
$125,000 (2% apprec. for largest homes)	$130,050	$135,300	$140,327	$146,462

Whether, in fact, the biggest house on the block will be a good buy for you depends on your needs, your objectives, and the home's price *relative* to houses more typical of the neighborhood. If you're asked to pay 50 percent more for a home that's 50 percent larger, you're probably not getting good value. If you can buy the larger home for just 10 percent more, then you're probably getting a great buy.

Don't simply avoid the most expensive homes. Instead, do a value comparison. Figure out how much more home you're getting for your money.

Just as important, compare the size and features of the larger home to your needs and objectives. If you have a large family or need space for a home office or more comfortable living, the most expensive home in a moderate-priced neighborhood might provide an economical way for you to meet these needs.

Also, consider the opportunity side of the ledger. Even if you don't currently need the extra size or features of the more expensive home, can you think of a use? How about an art studio, library, or work space? Could you rent out a room or two or maybe convert part of the home into an accessory apartment or mother-in-law suite?

Think income potential. Think affordability. You might be looking at a three-bedroom, two-bath house priced at $115,000. With 10 percent down, the mortgage payments on this home would run around $723 a month (7.5 percent, 30 years). Now say you discover a five-bedroom, three-bath house in the same neighborhood. You can buy this larger house for $135,000. With 10 percent down, payments on the larger house would cost $849 a month.

You may not need this extra space nor want to stretch your budget to come up with another $126 a month. But what if the larger home is designed (or remodeled) so you could rent out those extra two bedrooms and a bath for $375 a month? With this income, you'd cut your monthly mortgage payments down to $474. Rather than costing $126 a month more, the larger home would actually cost $249 a month *less* than the smaller house. Yet you would still enjoy three bedrooms and two baths for your own use.

In most instances, you're not wise to *build* the biggest and best home in the neighborhood. The prices of the smaller houses will bring down the value of the more expensive home. Whether you should buy the most expensive home (as a resale) poses a much different question. The answer depends on your needs, objectives, and how much more (or less) the larger home will cost each month. So don't automatically exclude the biggest or the best. Relative to the smaller homes, you could be passing up a bargain.

Mistake No. 24:   *I'd never buy a condominium. They make poor investments.*

Lesson: *Properly selected, condominiums can yield very good returns.*

In 1986 Paul Maglio bought a two-bedroom condominium located near Boston Harbor. He paid $120,500 for the unit. At the time Paul bought, 200 other potential buyers were registered on the complex's waiting list. Everyone wanted in on the sure-fire investment opportunity. With appreciation rates running at 2 percent a *month*, condominiums were the geese laying golden eggs.

Today the story's a bit different. Throughout Massachusetts, other states in New England, New York City, much of the Southwest, and Southern California, many condominium (and co-op) prices have fallen 30 to 70 percent off their 1980s peaks. Bruce Hopper, another Bostonian who lost a bundle on his condominium, sadly regrets his decision to buy. "It's too bad," Hopper says, "because condos were the ideal situation for a lot of people—first-time homebuyers who wanted the American dream. But it didn't pan out and now we're stuck."

With experiences like these in recent memory, many potential first-time homebuyers hesitate to buy a condominium. They'd rather stay put in their rental apartments than take a chance on getting "stuck" with a condo that can't be sold for anywhere near its purchase price.

These fears (or at least concerns) are justified. But as with all other investments, you should weigh potential risks against potential returns. Simply dismissing condos as "poor investments" without looking closely at the specific market opportunities that exist in your area could be a mistake.

It is true that, since the early to mid-1970s, many different condominium markets throughout the United States have seen their prices escalate wildly and then nosedive. Between 1973 and 1975 condo markets crashed in the Southeast, especially South Carolina and Florida. After a steep run-up in condominium prices in Chicago in the late 1970s and early 1980s, condo prices there fell more than the 1987 stock market crash. Between 1978 and 1983 many condos in Dallas and Houston tripled in value. By 1987 these same units were selling for 50 cents on the dollar. From the early to mid-1980s to 1988, Boston condo prices shot up without restraint. By 1989 the market had hit the skids. By 1993 nearly one-half the condominium homeowners associations in the state of Massachusetts were approaching insolvency. In the Burbank

Street complex in Boston, units that originally sold for $50,000 could hardly be sold for $5,000.

That's the bad news. But let's turn to the bright side for a moment. First, in nearly every case, the major groups of condo buyers who have lost money have been those who bought within a year or two of the top of the market. Longer-term owners nearly always have come out ahead. Second, condo owners who could see the crash coming and sold out near the top of the market often made tens of thousands of dollars. Third, buyers today who can learn to spot opportunity (and smell potential danger) stand to make good profits throughout the remainder of the 1990s. By learning the lessons of history, you can reasonably judge whether condo prices in your area stand a good chance of going up (or down). To spot opportunity here are the signals to look for:

1. Nearly everyone is pessimistic about future appreciation rates. (Yes, contrarians frequently do make money.)

2. The monthly after-tax payments for principal, interest, property taxes, insurance, and homeowner fees total less than monthly rentals on comparable apartments. In other words, you can own cheaper than you can rent.

3. The market values of the units are substantially below the cost of constructing similar new units. (See Mistake No. 31.)

4. Vacancy rates for rental apartments are less than 5 percent.

5. Local economic indicators (number of people working, retail sales, new car sales, bank deposits, new business starts, etc.) are beginning to show increasing strength.

6. The condo units you are considering enjoy some *unique* and *highly desirable* advantages (design, views, location).

7. Very few new apartment or condominium complexes are being built or planned. No major conversions of apartments to condominiums are under way or planned. Government restrictions limit apartment conversions.

8. Relative to single-family homes, condo prices (especially when calculated on a price per-square-foot basis) are low.

9. The condo complex you are looking at is stable: strong financial reserves for repairs and replacements; no pending litigation; very few units occupied by renters (fewer than 20 percent is good, less than 10 percent is excellent); relatively little turnover of owners and residents; well-maintained common areas; and harmonious relations among owners.

The absence of any of these 10 factors can stand in the way of increasing condo prices. History shows, however, that in most cases, a precipitous fall in prices usually is foreshadowed by one or more of these danger signals.

1. A collapse of the local economy.
2. Large numbers of apartments being converted to condos, especially when accompanied by very easy qualifier financing.
3. Large amounts of new condo or apartment construction.
4. The monthly costs of owning greatly exceed the monthly costs of renting.
5. More than 40 percent of a complex's units are investor owned and occupied by renters (or even worse, vacant).
6. Everybody "knows" values are going up at least 10 to 15 percent a year. The market is rampant with speculation.

Perhaps more than at any previous time, the late 1980s and early 1990s taught lenders, investors, and overly optimistic homebuyers that a condominium isn't a printing press for money disguised as a place to live. With most speculation now squeezed out of the market, condos in many cities once again offer good long-term investment potential. Remember, too, that owning a condominium protects you against future rent increases. (See Mistake No. 1.) Even ignoring appreciation, if you can own for less than you can rent, your condominium will yield a very favorable financial return. Plus, by paying down your mortgage balance, you will build up your net worth with home equity. And a condominium can help you escape from renter's jail. Today, in most cities throughout the United States, owning a well-selected condominium makes much better economic sense than renting.

Mistake No. 25: *IBM never lays anyone off, do they?*

Lesson: *Never buy a home without evaluating the emerging strength (or weakness) of your local economy.*

Think about these past events: In 1972 the Club of Rome, a group of world "experts," got together in Rome, Italy, and fed a bunch of numbers into a computer. Their output resulted in a study called *The*

Limits of Growth. Without zero population growth, this study concluded, the world would soon run out of resources, especially food. Famine was imminent.

Following logically from the conclusions of this study, billions of dollars were invested in U.S. farmland. Within a few years, farm prices jumped from $1,000 to $4,000 an acre. Banks, investors, and farmers rushed in to take advantage of the predicted economic strength of the farm belt states. Profits, it seemed, were there for the taking.

In 1982, after several years of OPEC-induced oil "shortages," the U.S. Department of Energy warned that "at current rates of production, the United States' reserves of petroleum will be used up in eight years—by 1991; natural gas reserves will be used up in 10 years—by 1993." Reacting to the sure profits to be made in the oil belt states, hundreds of billions of dollars flowed into Texas, Oklahoma, and Colorado real estate.

In 1989, as reports of New England's slide into recession caught national attention, homebuyers in Southern California lined up to buy homes as fast as they came on the market. Multiple offers became commonplace. Eager prospects for new homes even camped at development sites while waiting for the kick-off of the sales campaign. "We were afraid that if we didn't buy now, we'd lose our chance forever," said Theresa Nham at the time of her purchase in May 1989. "Forget New England. Southern California's economy is too diversified to suffer a downturn. Home prices here always go up."

In one sense, of course, history proves Theresa correct. Home prices have always gone up. But she should have added "over the longer run." In the short run, home prices can fall. The crash of a local economy can bring home prices down. And such a crash is all the more likely when speculation runs amok, as it did in the farm belt, the oil belt, and, more recently, the defense belt. As is now well known, even IBM can hit hard times and lay people off.

Looking back, it's easy to see that too many homebuyers have focused on the economic present—or, even worse, carried overly optimistic projections into the future as far as the eye can see. To prevent this mistake, before you buy, check the strength of your local economy. Is it stable and growing steadily? Does it show signs of weakness? Is it exploding with speculation?

What do the signals indicate?

- Are unemployment claims increasing or decreasing?

- Is help-wanted advertising in the local newspapers expanding or contracting?
- Is credit becoming more (or less) available for local businesses?
- Are office building occupancy rates and rents increasing or decreasing?
- Are used car prices (especially for the luxury or more expensive models) increasing or decreasing?
- Are bankruptcies of local businesses decreasing or increasing?
- Are home prices increasing moderately or have they been going up by 12 percent a year or more for the past two or three years? Are home prices falling?

Throughout the 1980s and early 1990s, nearly every area of the country—rust belt, farm belt, oil belt, sun belt, defense belt—experienced some type of economic downturn. Now, as we move toward the year 2000, each of these areas seems to have regained its path of economic growth. Overall, you can expect the remainder of the 1990s to bring steadily increasing home prices.

But short-term exceptions will occur. So don't simply assume your area's economic future. Investigate the facts. Nearly all areas go through periods of ups and downs. If the short-term economic outlook for employees in your area does seem shaky, it might be sensible to delay buying. Or you might especially focus on finding a growth neighborhood, a bargain-priced home, or a home where you can create value through improvements.

Mistake No. 26: *With all the new construction, we thought the economy was really booming. Home prices had to go up.*

Lesson: *Large amounts of new construction (homes, apartments, office buildings) often signal boom, then bust.*

When General Motors announced its plans to close the Buick plant in Flint, Michigan, and lay off several thousand auto workers, you didn't need a Ph.D. in economics to know home prices in Flint would take a plunge. But too much new construction in an area also can temporarily depress home prices. Somewhat deceptively, though, excessive new construction often creates a boom before it creates a bust. Apart from the contraction or expansion of an area's basic economy, the construction cycle itself can send home prices both up and down.

To see this cycle in action, ask yourself: Why do builders build? To make a profit, right? So as home buying increases and home prices rise, builders start constructing more homes and apartments. This construction and sales activity create more jobs for real estate agents, real estate attorneys, accountants, environmental impact specialists, site engineers, architects, electricians, carpenters, plumbers, suppliers of building materials, loan officers, and all the other people who benefit from home building and home buying. All this new construction also creates a demand for office space as businesses and professional firms expand. This brings in the developers of new office buildings. More construction-related jobs bring in even more demand for homes. Home prices continue to increase. Anticipating higher profits, builders continue to build more homes and offices to meet this growing demand.

Yet all booms end. Sooner or later, depending on the local levels of wages and employment, builders overshoot their market. Their inventories of unsold homes begin to increase. Office building vacancies climb. Developers cut back on their building. Workers are laid off. Incomes fall. Demand for homes falls. Builders have to cut prices or offer special buying incentives.

Newspapers take notice. Journalists talk up the weakening market. They find people to interview who are in financial trouble. They quote media experts who say a home is no longer a good investment. Resales of existing homes begin to weaken. Time-on-the-market figures show that homes are taking longer to sell. Prices for existing homes soften. Many potential buyers put their plans on hold. They want to wait and see. They ask themselves, "Why buy today if prices will be lower tomorrow? Besides, maybe our jobs and income aren't as secure as we thought." Both builders and potential buyers begin to fear economic uncertainty.

With the market slowdown, homes can no longer be sold for prices high enough to cover the costs required to build them. Many builders see red ink instead of profits. Lenders shut down their credit lines. Acquisition, development, and construction (ADC) loans become more difficult to get. Lenders also tighten their credit standards for home buyers. The housing boom becomes a bust.

Yet even as this slowdown is happening, population continues to grow. People get married. Children are born. Workers who have been laid off find new jobs. Recent college graduates begin their careers and start earning a monthly income. Businesses and factories that have closed are reopened by other companies. Entrepreneurs create new businesses. Total employment and wages begin to improve.

These economic changes don't just happen. Nor are they caused primarily by government programs. They occur because people who get hurt by economic downturns figure out ways to get back on their feet. Better circumstances and a more confident outlook means more people buy homes. Prices begin to firm up. Still, builders don't rush into new construction, for as economic recovery takes hold, construction costs tend to rise. Land, lumber, and building materials become more expensive. Cost-increasing safety and environmental regulations are tightened. Cities impose impact fees on new homes to pay the costs of needed roads, schools, parks, and other municipal facilities. Before builders really gear up for large amounts of new construction, they must wait for more homebuyers to continue pushing prices up to higher levels. That's the only way builders are able to cover the now-higher costs of construction.

As recovery takes hold, it's not just new homes that cost more. More upward pressure is placed on the prices of existing homes. As new homes become more expensive to build, the values of existing homes are pulled up along with the higher costs of new construction. When homebuyers, home sellers, and builders regain their confidence in the future, journalists change from pessimists to optimists. They begin to write articles more favorable to home buying. More renters decide to start visiting open houses and calling Realtors for help. Stories of multiple offers are heard. Waiting lists are required for presales of new home developments. Home prices move up by 5 to 10 percent or more. A new cycle is off and running. Reduced building during down cycles, increasing construction costs, and pent-up demand by wait-and-see buyers combine to ratchet home prices up another notch.

By understanding how this construction cycle typically works, you can avoid the mistake of buying with unrealistic expectations. Absent extraordinary local job growth and land shortages, home prices can't increase at rates of 10, 12 or 15 percent a year for extended periods of time. When escalating home prices become the chief topic of conversation at cocktail parties and office get-togethers, you can safely bet builders from throughout your region will be lured into the market with hopes of easy profits. More builders mean more homes for sale. Eventually, more homes for sale means a temporary decline (or leveling off) of home prices.

Buying near the top of the price cycle doesn't necessarily mean you've made a mistake. Over time, history has generally shown that "buying now" beats buying later.

Too many people who wait for the "best time" to buy end up procrastinating for years while they watch home prices ratchet up to higher and higher levels. In good times they say "prices are too high." In down markets they say "the economy's too uncertain." They always find an excuse to hesitate and avoid commitment. So "buying at the top" clearly beats perpetual procrastination.

However, if market signals do indicate the market is slowing, to prevent this mistake develop a cautious buying strategy. Don't use wildly creative (and dangerous) financing. Don't base your purchase on the belief home prices are going to double in four years. The homebuyers who have been hurt most by market downturns are those who have unrealistically stretched their finances and inflated their expectations.

Mistake No. 27:   *We're not buying now. The newspapers say home prices are falling.*

Lesson: *Interpret reports of home price decreases (or increases) carefully. Often such reports don't mean what they seem to mean.*

Have you seen any of those newspaper articles headlined "Home Prices Fell 8 Percent Last Year," or maybe "March–June Home Prices Up 15 Percent Over Same Period a Year Ago." If you have, don't put much faith in them. Chances are neither of these statistics is right.

In reporting home price increases or decreases from period to period, most newspapers and magazines incorrectly cite median price figures. The median price, however, tells nothing about the actual appreciation (or depreciation) of home values. The median sets a midpoint: Half of the homes sold for more and half the homes sold for less than the median price.

In periods when most homebuyers are buying lower-priced properties, the median will fall. In periods when upscale buyers pour into the market, the median price goes up. Median-price figures can tell you which price segments of the market are most active. But don't conclude that actual home values are moving at the same rate—or even in the same direction—as the median.

"Prince George's County [last year] showed the healthiest apprecia-tion of any market," writes Jacqueline Salmon in the *Washington Post*. "The *median* [emphasis added] price of a single-family house, includ-ing townhouses, rose to $133,750." Did homes in Prince George's County actually appreciate? If so, did they appreciate by 15 percent? To answer these questions correctly, you would have to compare sale-resale data for the same (or similar) homes. The median won't tell you.

By mixing up changes in median prices with appreciation (depre-ciation) rates, many reporters like Jacqueline Salmon unwittingly mis-lead their readers. I've often talked with potential homebuyers who believed home prices were falling, when prices were actually increas-ing or, at worst, holding strong. During the early 1990s downturn in the San Diego market, for example, many renters feared buying be-cause they thought home prices had stumbled. At the higher price levels ($500,000 and up), both prices and sales volume had headed down. Reflecting these changes, the median selling price of homes also fell. At the entry level ($125,000 to $175,000), though, home prices between 1989 and 1993 held steady and maybe even strengthened a bit. With improving mortgage affordability, savvy first-time buyers kept the low-end market reasonably strong (as contrasted to San Diego's sagging local economy).

On the other hand, when you fail to interpret reported price figures carefully, you also could conclude that home prices were appreciating faster than they really are. Because at some point along the way to full economic recovery, more move-up buyers will come back into the market. As upscale sales activity increases, the median price could quickly jump 15 to 30 percent. But without looking at sale-resale price data, it would be a mistake to conclude home values had actually jumped that much.

Overall, don't let median prices mislead you. Get the facts about homes, neighborhoods, and price ranges. Ask your Realtor to show you the actual trends in selling prices for specific types of homes. With facts instead of averages, you'll develop a better buying strategy.

Chapter 3

Valuing Your Home

Mistake No. 28: *We thought we got a real bargain. Our house was listed $20,000 below other houses we looked at in the neighborhood.*

Lesson: Don't compare homes on the basis of listing price.

When you start shopping for a home, your natural tendency may be to rank homes as a "good buy" or "overpriced" on the basis of their listing prices. Say your real estate agent shows you three similar homes in a neighborhood. One is listed for sale at $172,000, another at $189,500; and the third at $163,900. Based solely on this information, the home priced at $163,900 looks like a bargain. You may tell yourself, "We should grab this one. The sellers are way under the competition." But hold on to your hat. Before you leap for the "bargain," do a little more investigating.

ALL HOMES MAY BE OVERPRICED

First, recognize that all the sellers may be asking too much. None of the three homes may actually be priced in line with the current market. In fact, some sales agents have been known to steer eager buyers to three or four greatly overpriced properties and then show the unsuspecting buyers a home that's priced $10,000, $20,000, or even $50,000 less than the others. "I've been saving the best for last," say these agents. "This house just came on the market. You'd be smart to put a contract in on it right away. Several other agents from the office are showing the home later today. This one will probably go fast."

Before you jump at the chance of a lifetime, verify the "bargain" by checking the most recent *selling* prices of homes in the neighborhood. As markets slow down, many home sellers fail to adjust their listing prices with the new market reality. That's one reason for the home seller lament, "Homes aren't selling." It's not that buyers aren't ready to buy. Rather, "homes aren't selling" because sellers have listed their homes with unrealistic expectations.

As a result, time on the market lengthens. A few sellers who are serious about selling eventually become educated about the market and begin to reduce their listing prices. Others, though, hang on hoping for a miracle. Although in every market you'll find some homes listed at the owners' dream prices, in slow markets overpricing almost becomes the norm. In those situations, you especially want to avoid using listing price as a guide to value.

SELLERS WILL SELL FOR LESS

Listing price can mislead in another way too. You know that most sellers will sell for less than their listing price: But how much less? The owner who is asking $162,500 may hold tight to that figure. The owners who have their home listed for $179,800 may become so panicked about the "slow market" or their need for quick cash that they'll take the first serious offer they get—even when that offer was $150,000.

Should you find an overpriced home you like, don't write it off. Probe the sellers or your real estate agent to learn how flexible (desperate) the sellers might be. Use market facts about the actual selling prices of neighborhood homes to lead the sellers out of their fantasyland. At first glance, a home listed at $20,000 less than another may appear to be the best buy. But what if you can get the sellers of the overpriced listing to come down $30,000? In that case, the highest priced listing may end up as the real bargain.

Mistake No. 29:   *We thought we got a real bargain. We paid $10,000 less than the appraised value.*

Lesson: *Never put blind faith in an appraisal.*

Many prospective homebuyers mistakenly believe the end-all of real estate valuation is an appraisal. To the uninitiated, a property is worth what the appraisal says its worth—no more, no less.

In their book, *Getting the Most for Your Home*, Dan Liebreman and Paul Hoffman tell home sellers, "Americans often believe what they see in writing far more than what they are told. A written appraisal for your home, showing its value as higher than your asking price, sitting on the dining room table . . . gives you the edge in the logical part of convincing a buyer of the value of your home. . . . work the appraisal to your advantage, then sell the house 'below appraised value.' Buyers will feel they are getting a bargain" (p. 242).

On numerous occasions when I've been looking at homes for sale, a seller or real estate agent has used this ploy. "Look at this," the agent might say. "We've got this home priced $15,000 below its appraised value. The sellers are moving out of town. To get a quick sale, they're willing to practically give their house away."

Maybe they are. But maybe, too, they've "worked the appraisal" to their advantage to make "buyers feel like they are getting a bargain."

Should you run into this type of sales presentation, here are several things you should know about appraisals and appraisers.

APPRAISALS HAVE TIME-LIMITED VALUE

Appraisals are like a no-refund airline ticket. At best, they're good for one date only. So, one of the first things you need to do is look at the date of the appraisal. If home prices are changing (up or down), an appraisal that's even a month or two old could already be out of sync with the market.

CONSIDER THE COMP DATES

Even more important than the date of the appraisal are the dates of the "comps," or comparables. Every home appraisal is based on the recent selling prices of similar homes in the neighborhoods. Ideally, these sales should have taken place within the past 90 days. Often, though, in slow markets no comp sales have occurred recently. In these cases, appraisers sometimes go back six months or a year for their sales data. Obviously, "stale" comps may not indicate today's value.

If appraisers do go back in time for sales price data, they are supposed to bring the figures up to date with a time adjustment. But without recent sales data, how are they to know how much to adjust the past figures? As a result, they don't. They simply use a p.f.a. (pulled from the air) adjustment. Because of these appraisal difficulties, you should seriously question any appraisal that's derived from out-of-date or time-adjusted market data.

APPRAISERS DON'T MEASURE VALUE

An appraisal is not a certificate of value. Nor do appraisers "measure" or "determine" a home's worth. An appraisal is one man or woman's opinion of the price buyers are likely to pay for a home. Naturally, then, since appraisals are opinions, the appraisal process leaves wide room for subjective judgments. As a buyer who is informed about the market, you should feel perfectly free to disagree with or refute an appraisal. Don't let a seller, sales agent, or appraiser intimidate you into accepting an appraiser's estimate. Use an appraisal as market information—not as "the answer."

MANY CONDITIONS LIMIT APPRAISALS

Appraisals include many limiting conditions. Although we won't go into most of them here, one that I will point out reads as follows: "The appraiser assumes there are no hidden or unapparent conditions of the property, subsoil, or structures which would render it more or less valuable. The appraiser assumes no responsibility for such conditions, or for engineering which might be required to discover such factors."

In other words, except for patently obvious defects, the appraiser values the home as if it were problem-free. If the appraiser can't see the defect, then for the purpose of the appraisal, the defect doesn't exist.

Or sometimes, even when the appraiser can see the defect, she may assume it doesn't exist. Several years ago I was interested in buying a house in Gainesville, Florida. I was dealing directly with the owner because she was a friend of a friend and hadn't yet formally listed the home for sale. The house was only four or five years old, well designed, located in a good neighborhood, and only a 10-minute walk from the University of Florida campus. The owner showed me an appraisal on the property that estimated its value as $85,000 to $88,000. Those figures were typical of the neighborhood.

However, there was one problem with the house. The lower level, which consisted of a three-car garage and an unfinished home office, had several long (18 foot) cracks running through it. The cement floor had buckled up much like large tree roots can buckle a sidewalk. I asked the owner, "What caused those cracks?"

"Oh, those are settling cracks," she said.

Settling cracks? Not likely. I called a home inspector to take a look at the problem. He knew the cause of the cracks right away. "This house is built on clay with an improper foundation," he told me. "Every time it rains heavy, the clay absorbs the water, expands, and literally pushes the house upward. Then, when the clay dries out, it contracts, and the house falls."

That didn't sound too good. So I called several soil engineers and building contractors. Repairing the problem would cost anywhere from $10,000 to $40,000. And those costs didn't include any warranty or guarantee that the work would be successful.

I'm a bit of a risk taker, so I told the owner about the problem. (Later I found out she already knew the real cause of the cracks.) I said, "Let's talk price. Given the serious and indeterminate nature of the necessary repairs, I'm willing to pay $60,000."

She balked. "Sixty thousand dollars? The appraisal says $85,000 to $88,000," she pointed out.

"Yes, but that's not considering the foundation and soil problem," I countered.

"Yes, it does," the owner argued. She then showed me in the small print where the appraiser had commented that the cracks in the floor could cause some buyer resistance. Therefore, a probable selling price would sit closer to $85,000 than $88,000.

I said, "That's nonsense. No one's going to pay $85,000 for this house." I then called the appraiser. "How could you discount the value of a house just $3,000 or so when the repairs could cost $10,000 to $40,000?"

The appraiser said repair estimates weren't a part of her job. "Besides," she added, "that home inspector you used is always too critical." To make an even longer story shorter, I got nowhere with the appraiser. The owner eventually came down in price to $80,000. But she did that only reluctantly. Again and again she referred to the "appraised value" of the house of $85,000 (or more). "At $80,000," she said, "you're really getting a bargain. Plus, I'm willing to offer good terms on the financing. (Of course, she had to carry back financing on the property because no financial institution would have touched it with its foundation defects so obvious.)

As you can guess, I passed on the deal. I'm not that much of a risk taker. But this experience shows perfectly how appraisers can pretend problems don't exist, even when they know about them. Just as important, it shows how an owner would mistakenly ignore the common sense of the matter in favor of wishful thinking. The owner had an appraisal that said the house was worth $85,000. To her way of thinking, any price less than that would be giving the house away. (My hope is she didn't find a naive buyer who failed to understand the limitations of an appraisal and the need to get a home's physical condition checked out by a professional inspector.)

VERIFY THE FACTS AND FIGURES

To be safe, you should check the arithmetic of the appraiser's calculations and the factual description of the appraised property. With the use of computer-prepared appraisals, appraisers have been able to cut down on their errors of addition, subtraction, and multiplication. Still, mistakes do occur. So taking a few minutes to verify the appraiser's arithmetic can be time well spent.

Beyond mathematical errors, though, appraisals all too often fall into the "garbage in—garbage out" trap. When appraisers are busy, they might go through eight to 12 houses a day. Also, some appraisal firms operate "factory appraisal shops." They use untrained, low-wage employees or appraisal trainees to perform property inspections. Then back at the office a licensed appraiser fills in the appraisal forms and signs off on the report.

No matter what appraisal procedures are used, though, there are many ways errors can slip into the process. I recently saw an appraisal that included errors in the following areas: the square footage of the home, the size of the site, neighborhood zoning, the floor plan of the house, and the arithmetic. That was truly a "garbage in, garbage out" one.

By cautioning you to verify the facts and figures in an appraisal, I'm not implying that most home appraisals are prepared incompetently. I just want you to recognize that checking both the accuracy and reasonableness of an appraiser's estimates is good insurance. Those buyers who naively accept an appraisal at face value are making a mistake. And these words of warning especially apply when an appraisal is presented as part of a selling effort.

Mistake No. 30:   *The appraiser didn't tell us home values were going to fall.*

Lesson: *More than likely, your appraiser, your lender, and your real estate agent will not warn you that home prices may be weakening in your area.*

In December of 1988 Maria and Jorge Olson were sitting in the living room of the home they were hoping to buy. Five other couples and individuals were also present. The home was listed for sale at $290,000. The sales agent for the owners came into the room. Nervous tension hung in the air. "We're going to start the bidding now," the agent said. Offers started flying. Pandemonium broke lose.

"It was really wild," Maria recalled. "Then, after everyone had had their say and wrote up their offers, the agent and the owners left the room. When they came back, we just knew we'd won. We were right. The owners accepted our offer of $310,000 with just a financing contingency. We celebrated that evening by going out to dinner at the most expensive restaurant in town. With home values increasing 30 percent a year, even at $310,000 we got such a great deal we felt rich."

Sadly, three years later Maria and Jorge were in divorce court. They needed to sell their home and hired an appraiser. His value estimate came in at $260,000—just about the same as the listing price that several real estate agents had suggested to the Olsons. (Several other agents had estimated much higher.)

To say the least, the Olsons were distressed and angry. They wanted someone to blame. They decided to sue their lender and the appraisal firm the lender had employed to appraise the home when they had bought it. That appraisal showed a value for the home of $325,000. The Olsons knew the current market was weak. But surely prices couldn't have fallen that much. The first appraiser must have overvalued the home. Or, if prices were really going to fall that much, the Olsons argued, the lender and the appraiser had a duty to warn them.

The Olsons lost the court case for two reasons: First, expert testimony showed that a $325,000 value estimate in late 1988 fit within a reasonable price range for the home. Although one could question the appraiser's judgment on several points, the appraisal itself contained no egregious errors. Second, the court ruled that appraisers weren't hired to predict the future. Estimates of market value apply only to the date of the appraisal. Neither the Olsons nor any other homebuyers should expect an appraiser, their mortgage lender, or even their real estate agent to tell them whether home prices are headed up or down.

Throughout the United States, the ruling in this case generally holds. With limited exceptions, homebuyers must make their own forecasts. Appraisers only describe the current market. Appraisers might believe, "The market is wild with speculation. Buyers are crazy. Within a year prices are going to fall faster than the stock market crash of '87." But unless asked, appraisers aren't likely to put these comments in their appraisal reports.

Or the opposite is also true. In performing a market value appraisal, an appraiser wouldn't comment, "This is the best market for homebuyers we've had in years. Home prices are sure to double within the next five years." You could ask an appraiser (or real estate agent) to give you his or her opinion about where the market is headed over the coming years. But for you to see the future as clearly as possible, look to the market signals that we discussed in Chapter 2.

Too many homebuyers think they are getting a great buy if they purchase their home for less than its current market value. However, in most instances, buyers should take their eye off the "bargain" they are getting today and refocus on the future. Ask yourself these two questions before you buy: (1) What market signals (or property features) indicate this home will be worth more tomorrow than it is today? And (2) what market signals spell D-A-N-G-E-R? (See Mistakes No.'s 24, 25, 26.)

Mistake No. 31:   *We didn't even think of calculating replacement costs.*

Lesson: *The cost to reconstruct a home at today's prices can give you a good idea where market values are headed.*

If you look on the back side of an appraisal form toward the upper right-hand corner of the page, you'll find a box for calculations called "Estimated Reproduction Cost New of Improvements." By completing this section of the appraisal report, an appraiser tries to figure out how much it would cost to build the home (house or apartment) at today's prices. After subtracting for depreciation on the home and adding in the value of the lot, the final result is supposed to reflect the current market value of the house.

Very few homebuyers, however, pay much attention to these types of cost calculations. Like appraisers, most homebuyers prefer to rely most heavily on the comparable sales method of estimating a home's value: A house is worth about the same amount as other homes in the neighborhood that have sold recently. In fact, most appraisers simply fiddle with numbers in the cost-approach-to-value section of an appraisal report so that they agree with the value estimate they come up with using the comparable sales approach. Appraisers believe a home is worth what someone is willing to pay. How much it costs to build doesn't matter.

For purposes of estimating today's market value, the appraisers are right. Reproduction costs don't matter much. But for predicting whether home prices are going up or down, reproduction costs matter a great deal.

When Suzy Wilson and Carrie Sloan bought their townhouse in the hot Dallas market of 1984, they paid $123,000 for an 1,100-square-foot, two-bedroom, three-year-old unit. That price works out to about $112 per square foot. Since the market of 1984 was booming, Suzy and Carrie's real estate agent had found quite a few comparable townhouse units that had sold recently. Based on the selling price of similar units, these young accountants got a good price.

But Suzy and Carrie focused too much of this market analysis on current and rapidly escalating home prices of the past year. In doing so, they missed two critical market signals: (1) The Texas oil economy was showing signs of slipping. (2) More to the point for our purpose here, townhomes similar to the units these women bought could be built at a total cost (including land) of approximately $85 a square foot. That meant condo developers could expect to construct new units, sell them at their market prices (over $100 per square foot), and make a profit (killing) of $20,000 to $30,000 a unit. Naturally, this fact did not escape the attention of condo developers. With banks and savings and loans shoveling money out to developers (who actually often owned the S&Ls), the condo market became glutted with newly built units. As the oversupply of condos ran head on into the weakening Texas economy, what had been a severe shortage of homes for sale quickly became a surplus. Condo prices crashed.

At the same time, similar cost-value imbalances were felt in the markets for new and existing single-family homes. First, market values rose far in excess of land and construction costs. Then, fueled by the optimism of rising prices and increasing profits, builders rushed in to build more homes.

You know the end of the story: Billion-dollar bailouts for banks and S&Ls.

The Texas experience was extreme. Nevertheless, the general market forces of rising prices, expectations of increasing profits, and overbuilding run throughout our economic history. And they will again. But you can help protect yourself against value losses by talking to a few builders, contractors, or knowledgeable real estate agents. Ask them what it would cost on a per square foot basis to reproduce the type of home you're thinking about buying. Then do some rough calculations. If after allowing for land (lot) value and depreciation, your home-to-be looks too expensive relative to its reproduction costs, then don't count on much short-term appreciation. When home prices are 25 to 40 percent higher than construction costs, home values can easily fall.

On the other hand, if market prices are too low to cover new construction costs, then builders won't build many new homes and apartments. As the local economy strengthens, growth in incomes, employment, and population will push home prices up.

At any specific time, market values can rise above or fall below a home's building costs. Over time, though, home prices nearly always keep pace with the costs of new construction. Today's costs of construction may not tell you much about today's home values. But, more than likely, they will signal whether home prices are headed up or down. If builders can't build at a profit, they won't build. When excessive profits are expected, too many builders come into the market. Increasing numbers of new homes for sale drives prices lower.

Mistake No. 32:   *We didn't pay much attention to lot value. We wasted $22,000 on remodeling.*

Lesson: *Before you buy your home, separate the value of the home from the value of the lot.*

When Jeri and Rod Craig bought their older, slightly rundown home, they had great plans for it. The home was located in a neighborhood where some larger and newer homes were valued upward of $450,000. The Craigs paid just $145,000 for theirs.

After moving in, the Craigs undertook a top-to-bottom remake campaign for their home. Doing much of the work themselves, they refinished all the hardwood floors, installed new tile and fixtures in the bathrooms and kitchen, added a deck, enclosed a porch, and gutted the kitchen's out-of-date cabinets and appliances. Through their redesign and renovation, they transformed the kitchen (their favorite room) into a contemporary chef's delight. Indeed, throughout the entire home, their creativity and pride of workmanship displayed itself in every detail. Admiring the fruits of their labor, the Craigs were confident their six months of toil and $22,000 of expenses would enhance their home's value by at least $50,000 to $75,000. At a price of, say, $200,000, their home's value still came in near the low end of the price range for the neighborhood.

Unexpectedly, the Craigs got to test their value-added theory sooner than they wanted to. Within a year of completing their home's make-over, Jeri received a great job offer from a law firm in another city. The Craigs decided to move. They knew the housing market had done well since the time they had bought. Sales activity was high. Values were up. Compared to the other (and relatively few) lower-priced homes in the neighborhood, the Craigs' home stood out as the best. Since several of these lesser homes had recently sold for $165,000 to $175,000, the Craigs decided to list their house at $200,000 and go for a quick sale.

Yet 30 days passed, then 60 days, then 90 days. Several offers came in at around $170,000, but the Craigs felt insulted. They kept pointing to the high quality of their renovation work. Potential buyers agreed but wouldn't increase their bids. Eventually, when the Craigs could delay their sale no longer, they sadly accepted an offer of $175,000—hardly enough to cover the cost of the home and their out-of-pocket expenses, not to mention all the work they had put in.

Why couldn't the Craigs fully profit by their home improvements?

Because prior to their renovation work, they didn't think about the value of their lot. When they paid $145,000, they didn't really pay for a home. That came free. They paid for the land. Three weeks after they moved out of their perfectly modernized 1,400-square-foot bungalow, a bulldozer came in and leveled it. In its place, the new owners began construction of their five-bedroom, four-bath, 3,600-square-foot home. The Craigs had misspent their time and effort on a home that was obsolete for the neighborhood.

In one sense, Jeri and Rod had underimproved their lot. A small remodeled house was not the highest and best use of the site. In another sense, they had overimproved their house. Since the house no longer fit the neighborhood, improving it wasted time and money.

Before you buy a home with the idea of remodeling, figure out whether your remodeled home will fit the neighborhood. You can put too much money into a home if you try to increase its value well beyond other nearby homes. And you can also put too much money into a home that's *undervalued* for its location.

When a site's value exceeds 60 or 70 percent of the total value of the property, be careful. More than likely, the house is functionally obsolete for its site. Most (or all) of the appreciation potential for the "home" lies in its lot value. That's not bad from an investment standpoint. But in such cases, add improvements to the house primarily for personal reasons. At some point in the future (depending on the strength of the housing market), the home may become a "teardown," regardless of its physical condition. In the Kerrisdale section of Vancouver, British Columbia, for example, perfectly good three-bedroom, two-bath houses of 1,600 to 1,800 square feet are being sold for $350,000 to $400,000. Within a year of sale, the "small" homes have been torn down and replaced by new houses of 4,000 to 5,000 square feet with values approaching $1,000,000 or more.

Finding a "low"-priced house in an upscale neighborhood can be a great way to get started in home ownership. But go cautiously with your plans for improvements. In many instances, it's your lot that's going to give you your appreciation, not your remodeled house.

Mistake No. 33:   *Those "comps" weren't really comps.*

Lesson: *When relying on an appraisal, verify the comparability of the comps.*

"When I bought my home," says Richard Gans, "I looked at the appraisal the owner showed me. I didn't know much about it. It looked okay. The other houses on the form sold for around the same price the owner was asking. I offered $10,000 less and eventually we compromised by splitting the difference. He cut his price by $5,000."

"It was only after I moved in," Richard continued, "that I learned the other houses in the appraisal were in a better school district. That didn't bother me because I don't have kids. What did make me mad was that houses in the better school district typically sell at a $15,000 to $20,000 premium. I paid the premium but didn't get the school district."

Richard's experience illustrates a specific instance of a more general homebuyer (and appraisal) mistake: The comp houses shown in the appraisal weren't really comparable. As a result, the appraisal value was misleading.

In theory, the comparable sales approach to value tells appraisers (or home buyers) to estimate the value of one home by looking at the sales price of other "comparable" homes that have sold recently. In practice, defining "comparable" and discovering recent sales of comparable homes can prove both deceptive and difficult. So whether you're using the comparable sales approach yourself or are relying on an appraisal, look for differences among homes that can make a difference.

1. Make sure the comparable homes are really in the same location. Especially when you're unfamiliar with an area, it's easy to overlook subtle differences in location such as school district, zoning laws, prestige, accessibility, quiet, proposed or planned changes (street widening, airport runway expansion, new apartment or commercial development), crime rates, insurance costs, or property tax rates. (See Chapter 4.)

2. The homes should be similar in size, architectural style, floor plan, amenities, and condition.

3. The lots of comparable homes should be about the same size, configuration, and value.

4. Ideally, you (or the appraiser) should find several sales of comp homes slightly inferior to the home you're looking at and several slightly superior. If you can say "This house is clearly worth more than these two houses, and clearly worth less than these other three houses," then you've set a minimum and a maximum value for your home. Avoid using comps that all sit on either the high side or the low side. By bracketing, you can get a much surer picture of a home's value. Be wary of appraisals that don't bracket the "subject" property between higher- and lower-priced comparables.

Even through this brief discussion, you can see why choosing comps involves a great deal of judgment and knowledge. Often it's not easy to definitely say one house is "inferior" and another "superior." When it comes to homes, subjective feelings, tastes, lifestyles, and personal preferences all play a part. In addition, what if no truly comparable homes have sold recently?

All these difficulties make it prudent for you to examine and carefully review any "appraised" values you make or rely on. There's plenty of room for error as well as reasonable differences in opinion. Looking at the sales prices of similar homes can help you (or an appraiser) make more informed estimates of value. But since ideal comps seldom exist, you'll frequently need to answer these two questions: (1) What differences (among homes) make a difference? and (2) How much difference do those differences make? These are two key questions you don't want to forget.

Mistake No. 34:   *We figured the swimming pool added more to the home's value than it really did.*

Lesson: *Beware of costly extras, room additions, and other special features.*

When you start looking at houses, you'll soon begin to notice many of those differences that make a difference. One house has an oversized swimming pool and patio, another a hot tub, and another a paddleball court. The home in Oakridge has a remodeled kitchen, the Fairfield house is larger because the owners converted the garage to a den. The Pine Meadows house includes new Bierber carpeting throughout the entire home.

How do you figure how much these differences add to the value of these houses? Unfortunately, there are no hard-and-fast rules. And that exposes you to the mistake of overpaying. If you find a home with a feature (or features) that really hits your hot button, you may get so excited about the pool, the big yard, the great room, the hot tub, or the remodeled country kitchen that you overestimate how much that feature is worth. Or even worse, you "buy the feature" more than you buy the home. In that case, you may end up with a great room you love and a house you don't like.

Although you can't price special features by simply plugging numbers into a calculator, the following guidelines can help you decide how much you should pay for costly extras, room additions, or special features.

1. Find out how much it would cost to replace the feature and then subtract for depreciation. If a swimming pool and patio could be built for $12,000 and are 10 years old, that pool should add no more than $5,000 or $6,000 to the home's value (assuming 50 percent or so depreciation).

2. How easily could the feature be added to the home? Adding a swimming pool is a lot of trouble. Adding a hot tub or new wall-to-wall carpeting throughout the house is relatively easy. You should pay less for features that anyone could duplicate easily in nearly any home.

3. What is the cost of the feature relative to the price range of the house? Expensive features (such as Bierber carpeting or Poggenpohl kitchens) don't add much value to low- to moderate-priced homes. "The owner just spent $18,000 for these new custom-made cabinets and SubZero appliances," says the real estate agent. "Yes, they're very nice," you respond. "But I'd have to pay to have them removed. They're too rich for me."

4. Does the feature preserve the basic style and integrity of the home? Or does it seem out of character? I recently looked at a delightful and well-kept late 1940s Craftsman bungalow. The owner (a single man) had remodeled the kitchen along the lines of a 1970s suburban tract home. To make matters worse, he had decorated and designed the master bedroom with mirrors, lighting, and fixtures that made it perfectly suitable for the exploits of Heidi Fleiss or the Mayflower Madam. Although costly, no economically sensible homebuyer should pay more than 10 cents or 20 cents on the dollar

for the bastardized features. (In fact, those features may have actually decreased the home's value.)

5. Does the feature appeal to most homebuyers in the neighborhood or price range? If not, you probably won't have to pay much for it. Without wide-based popularity, it's not a selling feature—and may even be a detriment. In other words, consider relative supply and demand. You're fortunate if the features you like are in high supply (most houses have small yards and you prefer a small yard), while most other buyers want large yards.

6. Don't forget to account for land value. Remember the Craigs (Mistake No. 32). If the present house on the site isn't the best use for that location, don't pay much extra for special features or a tiptop condition. You could be wasting your money.

In valuing the pros and cons of "differences that make a difference" among homes, there's one more thing you should know: Appraisers may drive by the comp houses listed in an appraisal report, but they don't typically go inside them or even walk around the house and the yard. When an appraiser says one house is worth $8,000 more than another home because it's in better condition, that figure's a guess.

The same thing is true for all the "adjustment" figures used in the comp sales approach to value that are shown on an appraisal report. These numbers don't come from the appraiser's informed judgment. They're either pulled out of the air, based on rule-of-thumb estimates, or derived from second- or third-hand sources (multiple listing data, property tax records, talks with real estate agents).

This standard operating procedure of appraisers introduces considerable potential for error into the appraisal process. How can an appraiser really know one comp home is in $8,000 better condition if she's never been inside it? She can't.

On occasion, when faced with an appraisal that lists large and numerous dollar adjustments for differences that make a difference, I've actually gone out and inspected the comp houses. I've knocked on the doors, told the owners what I would like to do, and in most cases I've found them cooperative. In fact, they're usually interested to learn what information the appraisal includes about their home and the other houses valued in the appraisal report. As often as not, I've found the appraisal rife with serious errors.

Although you might feel uncomfortable asking strangers to let you in their homes, at least drive by the comps. Get an impression of the homes and the surrounding neighborhood. You might even talk to the real estate agent(s) who handled the transaction. (Remember comp houses are homes that have sold recently.) Whatever you do, don't casually accept an appraiser's figures. They're seldom based on his or her firsthand knowledge.

Mistake No. 35:   *We looked at selling prices but still overpaid.*

Lesson: *Discover the facts behind the selling prices.*

"We thought we were getting a really good deal on the house we bought," says Steve Rizzoli. "My brother and I knew the house three doors down had sold for $98,200 six weeks ago. Our house was about the same size and looked nicer on the outside. In addition, our house had a fireplace and a peek-a-boo view of the mountains from the upstairs front bedrooms. Based on these things, we were really happy to get ours for $100,000."

Later, though, Steve and his brother learned not all selling prices are created equal. The house three doors down did sell for $98,200. But to get that price the sellers had agreed to pay most of the buyers' loan closing costs, contribute $2,000 toward an interest-rate buy-down, and escrow money for a new roof. Together, these seller concessions were worth around $7,700.

In transactions more typical of the Rizzolis' area, seller concessions ranged between $1,500 and $2,000. So, in this instance, the sellers paid around $6,000 more than normal. Although the purchase contract showed a price of $98,200, the buyers actually got the house for an effective price of around $92,000. When the Rizzolis compared their home's cost of $100,000 to the $92,000 price their neighbors really paid, they no longer felt they had gotten a bargain. In fact, they felt they had overpaid.

Recent selling prices of nearby homes can give you a good idea of the price you should expect to pay for your home. Yet don't accept these numbers without question. Sometimes there's a story behind a home's sale that has pushed the selling (contract) price above or below the home's market value. Consider these questions.

1. Has either the buyer or seller been pressured by time or other circumstances? Sellers who need money fast may sell below mar-

ket value. Buyers who need a quick move-in date may pay more than market value.

2. Does the sale price include any of the seller's personal property, special fixtures, or home furnishings? The sellers may not be willing to part with the $2,500 crystal chandelier in the dining room—unless the buyers up their price accordingly. The same thing is true for the custom-made draperies, the kitchen and laundry appliances, the antique grandfather clock, or the basement workshop fully stocked with tools and equipment. If any of these items becomes a part of the sale, it also may become a part of the price.

3. Was the sale at arm's length? Whenever parties to a transaction are friends or relatives, the selling price may not tell the full story. More than likely, parents selling to their kids won't insist on top dollar.

4. Was the transaction handled by real estate agents? Buyers and sellers who rely on real estate agents tend to be better informed about the market. Their transaction prices are more likely to reflect market values. On the other hand, sellers or buyers acting on their own are more likely to sell for too little or pay too much.

5. Does the sale involve owner financing or other seller concessions? Cash-short buyers may agree to pay more for a house if the sellers help with the financing or pay part of the buyer's loan closing costs.

6. When did the sale actually occur? Often, the sale date recorded in public records or multiple listing files is the date of closing. That's the date money changed hands and the home's title transferred to the new owners. But for purposes of setting sales price and terms, the actual contract date could have taken place months earlier.

In stable markets, time differences of several months needn't cause much concern. In changing markets, however, a difference of several months can really mislead you. As a check, ask your Realtor to tell you the date the contracts were signed for the comparable home prices you're evaluating. Then ask whether the market seems to be changing. Are the inventories of unsold homes growing? Are homes taking longer to sell? Is there an increasing gap between listing price and offering prices? Has buyer traffic been dropping off at open houses?

By asking these kinds of questions, you can guard against buying into a slowing market with unrealistic expectations. When markets are changing, look beyond past selling prices because they won't tell you all you need to know to make a purchase offer.

Mistake No. 36:   *The sellers named the price, we named the terms.*

Lesson: Never agree to pay more than market value for a home unless you fully weigh the risks.

In the wild California housing market of the early 1980s, buyers and sellers were doing nearly anything they could to make a sale work. With mortgage rates at 14 to 16 percent, few buyers could qualify for bank financing. That left buyers with nowhere to turn except to the sellers. "Creative financing" became the norm. There were seller seconds, wraparounds, balloons, third and fourth deeds of trust, lease-options, and land contracts.

The commonplace rule of home buying was "You name the price, we'll name the terms." As long as buyers could handle the cash-down and monthly payments, they didn't care about the price. Operating with a late 1970s inflation perspective, buyers figured even if they overpaid, tomorrow's appreciation would bail them out and still leave room for a healthy profit.

By 1982, though, the tide had turned. California home prices had stopped their spiral of appreciation. Homeowners who tried to refinance to pay off short-term seller financing found they owed more than their homes were worth. Other who had relied on creative financing and lost their jobs or for other reasons needed to move also fell between a rock and a hard place. They couldn't afford to make their monthly payments and they couldn't afford to sell.

Here's how these and thousands of other homebuyers since the early 1980s have made this mistake: In most (but not all) instances, the buyers were cash short or for some other reason couldn't qualify for bank financing. The would-be sellers and financiers frequently had put their home up for sale at too high a price. This combination offered a perfect opportunity for a match. The buyers say, "Okay, we will agree to your price of $149,000 if you will accept $5,000 down and monthly payments based on a 30-year mortgage at 6 percent interest. After the first three years, we'll refinance and pay off the balance we owe you."

The sellers accept. They got their $149,000 price (for a home actually valued around $130,000). The buyers got the terms they wanted. Unfortunately, three years later the home's value has risen to just $140,000; mortgage interest rates are approaching 10 percent; and the buyers haven't been able to save as much as they had hoped. The buyers can't come up with the money they need to make good their promise to the sellers. They face foreclosure and eviction. The thrill of being able to have bought their first home turns into worry, fear, and sleepless nights.

Does this mean you should never trade price for terms? Not necessarily. But if you do, anticipate the downside. Don't expect unrealistic appreciation; don't count on mortgage interest rates falling; don't figure you're going to save more money from your paycheck than you normally save. Do put a clause in your contract with the sellers that extends your payoff date should the housing market or mortgage market go against you.

Most important, know the true market value of the home you're buying. Especially in hot markets, some homebuyers have jumped into a deal so eagerly, they didn't even stop to think how much premium they were paying for the sellers' liberal finance plan. As a minimum, then, whenever you offer (or a seller offers you) easy terms, know what it's really costing you. How much difference is there between your offering price and the home's actual cash price?

Mistake No. 37: *Everything looked like a bargain.*

Lesson: *When moving from a high-cost area to a low-cost area, take care to recalibrate your sights. Avoid overpaying.*

If you are moving from, say, San Francisco or Boston to Memphis or Phoenix, get set for a great surprise. When you first start looking at houses, you won't believe your eyes. "Four bedrooms, three baths, pool, den, and a half-acre lot—all for $169,900. Unbelievable!" You'll begin to think all the sellers have gone crazy. "Better act quick, this house is a steal. The owners must not know what they are doing."

Filled with excitement about the bargains everywhere, you unfortunately may lose your critical awareness. You'll mentally compare the houses you're looking at to the price of houses back in your previous hometown. Since compared to your last city, all the houses are priced so low, you run the danger of overpaying.

To avoid this mistake, take special care to get good local market information. Check selling prices, terms of sale, market conditions, and neighborhoods very carefully. Put the home prices in Boston or

San Francisco out of your mind. Recalibrate your sights. Stay focused on Memphis or Phoenix. Work with a real estate agent who's committed to helping you find the best deal for your needs, budget, and the local housing market. That $5,000 or $10,000 you save by careful shopping and negotiating could pay for a long-remembered Hawaiian vacation.

Mistake No. 38:   *I didn't buy anything. All the houses were grossly overpriced.*

Lesson: *When moving from a low-cost area to a high-cost area, recalibrate your sights. Don't pass up a bargain.*

When moving to (or living in) a high-cost housing market, you may tell yourself, "Home prices here are outrageous. Everything is overpriced." You talk with other people. You read newspaper articles lamenting the housing crisis. You see articles quoting experts who say homes are no longer a good investment. You hear politicians proclaim something must be done: "Only 18 percent of our young families can afford to buy their own home." Even more depressing, you know friends or family in Des Moines who just bought a nice three-bedroom, two-bath ranch for $89,500.

With all these influences and comparisons telling you homes are overpriced, it's easy to develop a negative mind-set. Sure you would like to own. You might even (sort of) plan to own. Yet each time you meet the relative high housing costs of the area face to face, you put your hands in your pockets and walk away. You keep thinking about those housing bargains in Des Moines.

Around the turn of the century, Russell Conwell, the founder of Temple University, became famous for his speech "Acres of Diamonds." The truth of his speech was so powerful, so enduring, and yet so simple that throughout the country and throughout his life, Conwell was called upon to deliver it more than 25,000 times.

Upon going through his speech and relating several case examples to illustrate his theme, Conwell would say, "My friends, that mistake is very universally made . . . I say to you that you do have 'acres of diamonds' right where you now live."

By "mistake" Conwell meant focusing on the "better" advantages or conditions that are thought to exist in other places, while passing up the opportunities (acres of diamonds) that lie in your own backyard.

Like Conwell, I confess to this mistake myself—and I've seen it made countless times by others. As to my own experience, in 1977, I moved from South Carolina to Vancouver, British Columbia. In South Carolina, I owned a new custom-built brick home in a very nice professional neighborhood. I sold the house for $51,000 (a fair price). In Vancouver, that $51,000 would buy a 650-square-foot one-bedroom condominium. To buy a small, single-family older home would cost around $90,000. Rather than appreciate what Vancouver had to offer, my mind kept drifting back to South Carolina where one could get twice the house for half the money. "These prices in Vancouver are ridiculous," I thought. And it was no trouble at all to find others who agreed. I did prefer to own, but everything simply looked too expensive. So, by default, I rented.

One year later, the owner of the house I was renting approached with an offer. "I've decided to sell," he told me. "If you'd like to buy before I list the house with a real estate agent, I'll give you a good price."

"I don't know. What kind of price do you have in mind?"

"Eighty-seven thousand," he said.

"Eighty-seven thousand!" I choked. "No thanks."

To this day, I can recall then laughing with a friend about the price the owner had proposed. My friend and I both easily agreed that $87,000 for a one-bedroom house was ridiculous. Someone would be a fool to pay that much.

Well, that "fool" was shortly found. The house sold several weeks later at a price of $91,000. The new owners completely rebuilt the house into a four-bedroom, three-bath home. Today that home would sell for around $750,000. The lot value alone would run around $450,000.

In misjudging this opportunity, my friend (also new to British Columbia) and I had compared the price of the one-bedroom house in Vancouver to home prices in the relatively low-cost cities where we had lived previously. By that yardstick, the price looked ridiculous. The man and this family, though, who bought the home enjoyed a difference perspective. They were from Hong Kong.

They realized Vancouver was a world-class city. Compared to Hong Kong, Tokyo, San Francisco, New York, or London, Vancouver prices were a bargain. Even better, the house they bought was located just a five-minute walk from the beach, a five-minute walk to shopping and restaurants, a 20-minute walk to the campus of the University of British Columbia, and a few miles (10-minute drive) to downtown

Vancouver and Stanley Park. In addition, the house enjoyed a panoramic daytime view of the mountains and English Bay and a nighttime view of the city lights of downtown Vancouver.

Yet, if asked at the time, I'm sure most people in Vancouver (not just newcomers) would have believed Vancouver home prices in general, and that home in particular, were overpriced. The press and nearly everyone else complained about the "housing crisis." No one spoke of great opportunities.

But great opportunities existed then, and they exist today. No matter how high home prices have climbed in your area (or the area you're moving to), relative bargains can be found. Compared to major cities throughout the world, American and Canadian home prices are still cheap. In any given metro area, there are still homes and neighborhoods well priced relative to others within the area. Most important, in the future, nearly everywhere today's home prices will be viewed as the good old days.

For the past six decades, our population has grown, our economy has grown, our exports have grown, total employment has grown, and home prices have grown. This decade is certain to yield the same types of increases. "No matter where you live," as Russell Conwell might tell you were he alive today, "if you give it half a chance, you'll discover acres of diamonds." With the right perspective, you can find a relative bargain.

Chapter 4

Location, Location, Location

Mistake No. 39: *We had such great views.*

Lesson: *Before buying a house with a view, determine whether the view is "protected."*

Heather Caldwell loved the location of the townhouse she bought. It was close-in, yet the development was completely surrounded by trees. "We all felt like we were living in a forest," Heather remembered. "At least for a while, that is," she added.

One year after Heather had bought her new unit, the townhouse developer began phase II of the project. The bulldozers arrived, down went the trees, and that was the end of Heather's view of the woods. But her disappointment didn't end there. Once the second phase of the project was sold out, trees along the road leading into the complex were cut. In their place, the developer built a strip shopping center topped off by an orange roof. "Within less than four years," Heather said, "we had almost totally lost our wooded views and tranquil setting."

In Chicago, Fred Poynter bought his one-bedroom condominium at Lake Point Towers because it offered spectacular panoramic views of the city from both his living room and bedroom. Three years later Fred's view had changed. Instead of the city lights of downtown Chicago, Fred looked straight into another high-rise. Not only had Fred lost his view, he had lost his privacy.

On the outskirts of Orlando, Florida, Fay and Willy Lange bought their home because its lot bordered a grove of orange trees. Then Central Florida was hit with back-to-back winter freezes. The orange trees were killed. Instead of replanting, the grower sold his land and moved his business farther south, to Homestead. Now the Langes' property backs up to another subdivision. Gone forever are the views and privacy the orange groves provided.

Before you buy a home with a view, check to see how well that view is legally protected. Do zoning laws, building regulations, or environmental restrictions keep someone from blocking or destroying your view? Too many homebuyers pay a premium price for a view home, only then to lose not only the view but also thousands of dollars of value from their homes. Although you can't get 100 percent protection because the government might change the protection laws, at least you'll know what chance you're taking.

Both Heather Caldwell and Fred Poynter mistakenly believed their views were permanent. Had they checked the zoning laws or developer's plans, however, they would have discovered the views were almost certainly temporary. Of course, the Langes couldn't have forecast back-to-back record-setting winter freezes. But a little investigation would have revealed to them that even before the killer freezes, many orange growers were abandoning their groves and selling to subdivision developers. With this knowledge, the Langes may have decided to look for better protection elsewhere, or they may have chosen to offer a lower price for the home.

No one should *assume* their view will last. Before you buy, estimate the probabilities, and adjust your price accordingly.

Mistake No. 40:   *We never saw the railroad tracks.*

Lesson: *Ask the sellers and your sales agent to disclose any disturbing noises in the neighborhood.*

"When we bought our house," says Rose Bailey, "all we saw in the backyard was an eight-foot-high wooden fence with tall bamboo growing in front of it. We liked the fence and the bamboo because it gave us so much privacy. We never thought to ask what was on the other side. After we moved in, though, we soon found out.

"Twice a night, every night, a loud house-shaking freight train comes roaring through at 2:00 A.M. and 4:00 A.M. The railroad tracks—we now know—lay just on the other side of our backyard fence."

Before she bought, Rose Bailey forgot to inquire about noise pollution in the neighborhood. Hundreds of thousands of homebuyers have made the same mistake because it's so easy to make. Even if you should visit a house three or four times before you buy it, how much time are you likely to spend in the home? Three hours? Four hours? At most, perhaps, five hours. You can't learn much about neighborhood noise pollution—trains, buses, trucks, aircraft flight patterns—in such a short amount of time. You must do some research. Ask the sellers. Ask your Realtor. Talk to neighbors.

I once bought a house located on a small road removed from noisy traffic. At least that's what I thought. As I soon learned, though, the small road was a major short-cut teenagers used to travel to and from their high school. Since my house was near an intersection with a stop sign, during the morning, lunch, and after-school hours, it often sounded like race trials for the national drags or Daytona 500 were being held right outside my door.

Like many other homebuyers, my visits to look at houses were primarily on the weekends. On Saturday morning the home was perfectly quiet. And this brings us to another reason it's easy to miss noise pollution. Quite often visits to a house occur at the very times noise pollution is least likely to create a noticeable bother.

You can physically inspect a house at nearly any hour of the day or the week. Its basic character won't change. The neighborhood's a separate question. The timing of your visit can make all the difference. So, if before you buy you can't camp out near the home for 24 hours a day for a week or two, do the next best thing. Vary the times and days you visit the home; and ask the sellers, neighbors, and your Realtor to fully describe and disclose any disturbing noises that may plague the neighborhood.

Mistake No. 41: *We bought into an upscale development that's moving downscale.*

Lesson: *Before buying into a new development, find out what type of homes the developer has planned for later phases.*

"Several years ago we bought our first home in an upscale new development," says Kiki Allison. "We paid $250,000 and invested five years of savings in our down payment. Now we've learned the developer is planning to build townhouses and smaller homes right next to ours. He plans to sell them for $125,000 to $160,000. We're afraid this will change the character of the development and make our home less valuable. We wouldn't have bought here had we known the subdivision was going downscale."

Kiki Allison is describing a not-uncommon complaint. Sometimes developers build the most expensive phase of a development first. The upscale homes create a prestige image for the project that makes it easier for the developer to sell the more modest homes that are built later. Naturally, buyers of these later phases are attracted to a development that's already noted for its fine homes, manicured lawns, safe streets, and driveways stocked with BMWs, Volvos, and Land Rovers. Just as naturally, though, the BMW crowd's not too enthusiastic about the "cheapening" of their neighborhood.

So this creates a problem: How can prospective buyers of early-phase homes guard against surprises that could "downscale" the neighborhood?

The first line of defense is to ask the developer. Usually, later phases of the development are planned before phase I sales begin. Also, try to determine whether the developer plans to "merge" the stages of the development. Will all homeowners share the same common area amenities (tennis courts, pools, parks, trails), or will each area enjoy exclusive use of its own facilities? Will the separate phases share a common entrance to the development? Will the lower-priced units be marketed under their own names, or will the total development go by the same name, or perhaps Windwood I, Windwood II, and Windwood III? Will the separate phases be organized into one combined homeowners association, or will each community have its own membership roster? Will the phases be visually and physically separated from each other by natural or artificial boundaries such as parks, lakes, creeks, trees, and major streets?

However, even though development plans may be *proposed* for later phases, seldom are they etched in stone. Over time, housing markets change. Move-up homes may sell fast for several years and then the market might slow. Starter homes might gain more popularity. In a changing market, plans for $300,000 homes may be scrapped in favor of $150,000 townhouses and maybe even some rental apartments.

As a second line of prevention, then, ask whether the developer's plans for later stages are subject to market changes. Or are the developer's options and prerogatives limited by zoning laws, deed restrictions, warranties, and representations to buyers in early phases, or a vote by members of the phase I homeowners association?

For example, in many developments, deed restrictions prohibit lot sizes of less than, say, one acre, or homes of less than 2,400 square feet. Laws or restrictions also limit housing densities—usually stated as so many units to the acre. Developers of condominiums, townhouses, and apartments typically push for densities as high as they can get them. On the other hand, home buyers in early phases prefer low densities in later stages.

As a rule, when you investigate a development, you'll find your best protection against downscaling lies with the deed restrictions. Deed restrictions are very difficult to weaken without a majority vote of all affected homeowners. Zoning and other land use laws give you some protection. But they're subject to change depending on the direction of the political winds. Warranties and representations from the developer concerning future plans suffer in effect because most developers won't make written promises—and you should *never* rely on the oral promises of the developer's marketing staff.

The marketing staff may give you a color brochure and show you scale models of how the development will look in five or 10 years, but don't pay much attention to this type of promotion unless it's backed up more formally in writing. Too many homebuyers who have relied on glowing visions painted by an enthusiastic sales staff have met later disappointment. In recalling or pointing to oral promises or promotional brochures, disgruntled homebuyers have on occasion won lawsuits against developers to prevent downscaling. But litigation is a last-ditch effort. It costs years of hassle and tens of thousands of dollars in legal fees. And you still might lose.

It's far better to avoid the mistake in the first place: Don't assume later phases of a development will fully complement and enhance the value of earlier phases. Investigate what protections the developer is actually offering.

Mistake No. 42: *When we bought our house, the land across the street from the subdivision was a cornfield. Now it's a concrete parking lot and shopping center.*

Lesson: *Always envision the future within your neighborhood.*

"I remember when we bought," says Aaron Vasko, "the neighborhood was quiet and you had no trouble pulling in and out of the subdivision entrance. Now, since the shopping center's come in, you might have to wait through two or three light changes, especially at the commute times or on Saturday when it seems like everybody in the world's out shopping."

No one can anticipate all the changes that might affect a neighborhood. Some changes, though, are easier to spot than others—if you know what to look for. As a starting point, look around for vacant or "underutilized" land. Are croplands beginning to seem out of place? Are there wooded areas of private property near other tracts that are already being developed? Are roads or streets being widened?

If you're buying into a city neighborhood, find out whether rates of homeownership in the neighborhood are increasing or decreasing. Are growing numbers of property owners renting out rooms or cutting up single-family homes into apartments? Are any of the single-family homes being converted to offices or retail use? Does the government own any nearby land? Does the federal, state, or local government plan to put up any public low-income housing nearby? Are the parks deteriorating? Is graffiti spreading? Are the number of vacant buildings increasing?

When you buy a home, you're also buying the future of the neighborhood and the surrounding areas. As the neighborhood goes, so goes your home's value. But investigating a neighborhood doesn't just mean looking at what exists today. It means trying to imagine what it will look like five or 10 years down the road.

Close your eyes and let your imagination carry forward from the present into the future. What types of buildings will sit on those vacant tracts? Will the streets and roads become more congested? Will property owners have improved their homes and landscaping? Have property owners and neighborhood residents joined together to work for positive change? Or have they been indifferent (or even destructive) to the character and appearance of the area? Relative to other neighborhoods and communities, will this one have moved up or down the scale of desirability?

Especially think about traffic congestion. Will it get worse? Can the present roads accommodate all the new development? Will other areas or neighborhoods become more (or less) accessible?

Some years back, in metro Columbia, South Carolina, the northwest corridor of the city running out along I-26 became the most popular area for new development. Homebuyers were scrambling to get their children out of city schools and into the suburban school districts. Relative to most other areas of Columbia, the northwest corridor was hot.

But each new subdivision created more traffic. Several of the key Interstate exits would back up for half an hour. To many potential homebuyers, the traffic congestion looked intolerable. So they started searching for other developments in less congested sections of the metro area. Within two years home appreciation in the northwest subdivision slowed. Appreciation rates in the less congested northeast and southeast areas picked up speed. In fact, within two years, home values in one southeast development that found particular favor jumped by 40 percent.

When evaluating neighborhoods, subdivisions, and communities, remember that change is a fact of life. Never assume the future will look like the present. The chances are it won't. So by trying to anticipate and envision the changes that seem imminent, you're more likely to avoid unpleasant "surprises"—and you might even be able to pick a star performer.

Mistake No. 43:   *It didn't even occur to me that on weekends and during the warm months, the place could turn into a zoo of wild kids and party animals.*

Lesson: *Try to find out if your neighbors' lifestyles are compatible with your own.*

Like many first-time homebuyers, Ann Hennig had thought about investing in a home off and on over a period of years. Yet indecision and procrastination conspired to keep her renting. Then, when Ann's landlord gave her a 30-day notice that he wanted to move back into the home where she had been living, Ann decided the time was right. She would buy a home of her own.

Pushing herself to act quickly, Ann found a townhouse that was priced right, spacious, located only five minutes from her office, and it could be bought with a low-down-payment VA mortgage assumption. Best of all, her mortgage payments (after tax deductions) would cost her less than she'd been paying in rent. Those were the good points.

After moving in, however, Ann discovered a few things she had overlooked: "Children screaming and riding their Hot Wheels, everyone blasting their favorite radio stations, barking dogs, and late-night parties—all these things came as a big surprise to me," says Ann.

How did Ann get herself into this kind of situation? Here's her account. "First of all," Ann continues, "I have to explain my own ignorance. I came from the neighborhood I had grown up in. I had known my neighbors all my life, and except for an occasional outburst, the neighbors were pretty set in their ways and were generally quiet and considerate. You could always count on peaceful afternoons and quiet evenings. Since I had never been faced with the problem of constant noise, it was not something I consciously thought about. It didn't occur to me the place could turn into a zoo of wild kids and party animals.

"Also, I moved into my townhouse in October when the children were in school, most of the neighborhood was working, the weather was cold, and not many people were outside. The few times I visited the premises before I purchased it, I didn't stay long and didn't hear any of the neighbors, or maybe I just came on relatively quiet days. Anyway, I didn't pay much attention.

"But something else contributed to the problem. It seemed like we had a sort of Gresham's law of neighborhoods working. Bad residents were driving out good ones. Since I came from a neighborhood where people rarely moved, I had naively assumed that the neighbors I had when I moved in would be my neighbors for many years to come. At least in the beginning I had relatively quiet neighbors beside me and in back. Within a year they were both gone. In their place came a divorced man who partied constantly indoors and out on his patio, and a young single woman behind me who played her stereo from 8:00 A.M. to 10:00 P.M.—I think to accompany her barking dogs.

"On top of all of this, parking was another problem. Each unit had its own assigned parking space. When I visited the units before buying, many of the spaces were empty so it looked like parking was plentiful. But, of course, most people had been at work. On the weekends and in the evenings it was a different story. Since most units had more than one car, parking was clearly inadequate. I was also soon to learn that most residents had a total disregard for someone else's assigned parking space. Sometimes cars were even abandoned. Repeated calls to the police were all in vain.

"Later when some of us who cared tried to put together a more effective homeowners association to develop and enforce stricter rules, we ran into a brick wall. Too many of the units were owned by absentee investors. Since they didn't live there, they couldn't have cared less about unruly neighbors. And they certainly didn't want to put more money into maintenance and upkeep of the property."

No doubt, Ann's negative experience sounds extreme. Nevertheless, it can't be emphasized too strongly: Try to determine as well as you can the compatibility, stability, and cooperativeness of your future neighbors. Ann's mistake is very common. She naively assumed her new neighbors would behave with the same consideration and friendliness that Ann had known in the neighborhood where she grew up. As she learned, to her regret, that assumption may run counter to the facts.

Mistake No. 44:   *These people were a bunch of snobs.*

Lesson: *If you want to socialize with neighbors, find out whether you'll fit in.*

In today's world of hectic schedules, easy transportation, and instant communication, our chief socializing may take place on a catch-as-catch-can basis with friends and relatives located across town or across the country. Unlike the past, today many of us seldom get together with neighbors—and we may not even know their names. The old notion of sipping morning coffee at the neighbors' kitchen table seems as outdated as the TV reruns of a 1950s family sitcom.

To Abe and Lucille Hoskins, though, the very idea of neighborhood meant neighborliness. That's the type of neighborhood they each had grown up in and had become accustomed to while raising their own children. Abe and Lucille were also a living example of the American Dream. Starting life poor, and lacking a college education, by their mid-forties Abe and Lucille had achieved an income of $90,000 a year and a net worth (primarily equities in rental houses) of nearly $500,000. Their level of income and wealth placed them near the top 2 or 3 percent on the income scale in their midwestern town. In economic terms, they were among the town's "well-to-do."

Yet Abe still worked at the steel plant, and whenever tenants moved, Lucille personally cleaned their rental houses. Following the model of Sam Walton, Abe drove an old pickup truck. Lucille bought her clothes at Kmart. The one extravagance they both wanted (and could certainly afford) was a home in Woodshire, the best upper-middle-income neighborhood in their city.

After much searching, the Hoskins found a Woodshire home they fell in love with. They put an offer in the first time they saw it. The house was exactly what they wanted.

Sadly, though, as Abe and Lucille were soon to discover, the neighborhood proved to be a great disappointment. Although in appearance and convenience it left nothing to be desired, in neighborliness it failed on every count. Not only did the neighbors seldom socialize with each other, they overtly snubbed the Hoskins with their unspoken attitude: "Since you're not professionals and don't have a college degree, you're not as good as us. We choose not to acknowledge your existence."

Many homebuyers could ignore this nasty attitude and go on with their lives. Not Abe and Lucille. They did not want to merely own a house, they wanted to feel like they were part of a community. That didn't happen. Within two years the Hoskins sold their "dream house" in Woodshire and moved back to their old home on South 14th Street (which they had kept as a rental). "Those people in Woodshire were a bunch of snobs," Lucille told her friends. "We didn't fit in."

Houses and lawns, trees and shrubs, streets and sidewalks, parks and playgrounds, schools and libraries, shops and restaurants, these are the parts of a neighborhood you can see. But look beyond the physical characteristics. Before you buy a home, find out who lives in the neighborhood. Is there a feeling of community? Where do the people work? What are their educational backgrounds? What are their ages? Are they primarily married or single? Do they have children? What are their lifestyles and attitudes? Are they neighborly? Do you think you will fit in? Does it matter? Had the Hoskins asked themselves these questions, they would have prevented their home-buying mistake.

Mistake No. 45:   *You're saying we can't build a fence around our yard! Isn't that unconstitutional?*

Lesson: State and local governments can regulate the use of your property down to the smallest detail.

The Fifth Amendment to the U.S. Constitution declares that no person shall be "deprived of life, liberty, or property, without due process of law; nor shall private property be taken for public use without just compensation." In addition, nearly all state constitutions include clauses similarly written to stop governments from encroaching on an individual's property rights.

In interpreting these protective clauses, though, courts have defined a "taking" very, very narrowly. In effect, courts have said governments may squeeze an owner's rights as tightly as they want—so long as an owner still enjoys some minimal use of the property. As Nicole and Brett Gates learned to their dismay, a prohibition against backyard fences by the Village of Inverness did not even come close to testing the "takings" clause.

Of course, government regulations can work either against you or for you. If your neighbor is planning to build a second story onto his home that will block your view of the bay, you'll be more than eager to remind him that the added height of his remodeled home will violate the zoning and building regulations. On the other hand, when you learn you aren't allowed to rent out the room above your garage to a local college student, you're very likely to feel government has gone too far. After all, isn't a "man's home his castle"?

In real life, there's nothing objective about government restrictions on property rights. Whether you're for or against them all depends on what you intend to do with your property and what you want to prevent your neighbors from doing. Nor are property rights and restrictions uniform among neighborhoods and communities. One neighborhood might encourage accessory apartments, another might prevent them. Jackson Heights might permit in-home businesses, Fairview may outlaw them. All this means that before you buy a home or a lot, you should investigate the types of government restrictions that will apply to you and your neighbors.

Consider what happened to Allan Funt, best known for his *Candid Camera* movies and television shows. Mr. Funt bought 1,200 acres of land near Monterey, California. He intended to build four buildings on the site: a house, a visitor's guest house, a barn, and a stable. The

California Coastal Commission (the "zoning" authority over the 1,200 acres) refused permission. Instead the commission allowed Mr. Funt to build just two structures and ordered him to grant the public a 300-acre scenic easement through the site. To top that, the commission further specified that Mr. Funt situate and landscape his home such that after dark, no passersby would be able to see the home's lights.

If you're lucky, you won't be regulated to the same extent the California Coastal Commission has regulated millions of Californians. But here are the types of restrictions you might face:

- Height restrictions. Most homes are limited in height. You may not be able to add a second or third story.

- Side yard, front yard, and backyard restrictions. Land use laws typically require a home to be set back a certain distance from each of the site's boundaries. You may not be able to build onto the house or garage.

- Floor area ratios. These regulations limit the maximum square footage of your home.

- Use restrictions. These laws may prevent you from operating an office or business from your home.

- Occupancy laws. These regulations may limit the number of people who can live in your home. On occasion, they also may prevent more than three or four singles from sharing a home.

- Rental unit prohibitions. You may not be permitted to rent out a basement suite or add on an accessory apartment.

- Energy conservation. These laws may apply to anything from window size and placement to retrofitting your toilets with water-saving devices.

- Nuisance ordinances. These might include virtually anything you do that annoys your neighbors or vice versa. Fence heights, barking dogs, overhanging trees, car parking, practicing musical instruments, public nudity (sunbathing au natural in your backyard)—the list could go on.

- Remodeling and renovation. Nearly any serious remodeling or renovation will require a permit and government approval.

- Historic preservation. Should you buy a historically significant home or a home located in a designated historical district, any changes you make to the home will have to conform to prescribed historical aesthetic and architectural standards.

Jason Shields, an Ohio Realtor, says that far too many homebuyers pay too little attention to zoning and building regulations. "They buy a home with big plans. Then they find out they can't do what they want to do. Because I can't give legal advice," Jason points out, "I tell them to talk over their intentions with a lawyer, a reputable contractor, or the city planner's office. But they forget or let it slide and end up disappointed.

"Sometimes it also works the opposite way," Jason adds. "By failing to check neighborhood zoning, they get all upset when an apartment building starts to go up two blocks over. Or maybe they don't like the idea of their neighbor operating a workshop out of his garage and parking four or five cars along the street. Either way, I try to emphasize the laws will help determine the character of the neighborhood. So they ought to make sure they get the protection they want yet not so restrictive as to interfere with their own plans. It really is a matter of finding the neighborhood with the right balance."

Mistake No. 46:　*No need to worry, those laws are never enforced.*

Lesson: Be wary of both nonconforming and illegal property uses.

More than likely, some of the homes you look at will not conform to the neighborhood's existing zoning laws or building regulations. It's not uncommon to walk into a home and find a built-on den that sits too close to the property line, an illegal basement rental suite, or maybe outdated (but not hazardous) wiring. If you question the real estate agent or sellers about the violation, they may say something like "Don't be concerned, those laws are never enforced." Cy Torre, though, found out differently.

Cy bought a four-unit flat in Waukegan, Illinois. It was his way of getting over the affordability hurdle to homeownership. Cy lived in one of the units and collected enough rents from the other three apartments to cover a big part of his mortgage payments and property expenses. At the time Cy bought the fourplex, the neighborhood was zoned single family and duplex. Cy knew his apartments violated the law, but so did a number of triplexes and fourplexes in the area. The seller told Cy, "There's nothing to worry about. It's been this way for years and no one's ever said anything."

So Cy bought the flats without investigating further. That was his mistake.

Cy had chosen this neighborhood because it was being revitalized. Recent buyers had begun to spruce up their homes, clean up the nearby park, and establish a neighborhood crime watch program. They also began to complain about parking.

Since this was an older neighborhood, many homes lacked garages and few had enough on-site space to park two cars. As a result, these younger recent homebuyers (who owned more cars than the previous homeowners) often found themselves driving around the block several times before they could find a parking space. Joining with other neighbors, they put pressure on the mayor to solve the problem.

Whenever some neighborhood group complains about inadequate parking, the first casualties are owners of homes with illegal suites or flats. "Get rid of these tenants and there would be enough parking spaces for us homeowners."

So that's how the mayor solved the problem. He sent investigators out to count mailboxes at all properties in the neighborhood. Owners with more than two boxes were cited for violating the zoning ordinance and ordered to bring their properties into compliance within 60 days. Cy not only had to spend $6,000 to remove kitchens and take out several walls, his rental revenues went down. Over the long run, Cy will probably benefit from these changes through increased property values in the neighborhood. In the short run, though, he suffered a near-fatal cash crunch.

In Cy's case, his building violations were illegal. Whenever you own a property that *illegally* fails to conform to existing zoning or building regulations, you run the risk that an enforcement campaign will force you to make costly repairs or renovations. (Lawrence Ginsburg, a New York City developer, was recently forced to remove the illegal top 12 stories of a 31-story apartment building he had constructed more than five years ago. In addition to losing the rental income of 12 stories, Mr. Ginsburg had to pay $1,000,000 for their demolition.)

NONCONFORMING USES

Not all noncompliance, however, is illegal. Often zoning or building regulations are changed and existing uses or buildings are "grandfathered." Once grandfathered, they become "nonconforming" uses, but not illegal. Yet nonconforming uses do pose two risks.

First, the governing powers may change their minds. If they choose, they usually can take away or phase out a grandfathered use. So political winds blowing from a different direction, or "offended" neighbors who raise a fuss, can lead a nonconforming use to a premature death. (In Palo Alto, California, for example, complaining neighbors forced the political powers to get rid of a nearby office building. In compromise, the owners of the offices were permitted a 15-year phase-out.)

As a second risk, you might lose permission for a nonconforming use if you suspend or discontinue it. Say you operate a home business that doesn't conform to existing laws but has been grandfathered. If you shut down your business for several months, you may not be allowed to reopen it.

I once owned a rental house that had a 60 amp electrical system that was grandfathered. Current building codes specified a minimum of 100 amp service. Unfortunately, the home suffered a small fire in which some of the wiring was damaged. But the building inspector wouldn't permit repair. Instead, he pointed out the law required me to completely rewire the entire house to comply with present standards. A $200 fire cost me $2,000 to repair.

Throughout the United States, as many as 50 percent of houses and small apartment buildings may violate some current zoning ordinance, building regulation, or environmental restriction. Especially if you're buying an older home, you may not be able to avoid these kinds of properties. Just don't buy blind. Try to discover the violations. Learn whether they're illegal or merely nonconforming. And think through what risks they might present.

As the risks grow bigger, your offering price should be lower. If you're expected to bear the risk of noncompliance, then the sellers should discount their price to make up for it.

Mistake No. 47: *We live in Naperville, but our kids can't go to Naperville schools.*

Lesson: Your address doesn't necessarily tell you where you live or the services you are entitled to.

The address of my current home is in Berkeley, California, and I receive mail service through the Berkeley post office. But for purposes of zoning, building codes, school district, and property tax rates, the house falls within the jurisdiction of Oakland, California. Highland Park, Texas, a self-contained high-income community within the city of Dallas, is well known for its high-quality schools. But if you live on the wrong side of the freeway that slices through Highland Park, your kids must attend the Dallas public schools.

In Naperville, a prosperous and growing suburb of Chicago, homebuyers have flocked to the new subdivisions being built south of town. Homes typically cost $150,000 to $300,000; but many of the buyers are surprised to learn they are not located in the Naperville school district. Rather, they're within the Wheatland school district. Although Wheatland's schools are reasonably good, most families prefer the more acclaimed programs of Naperville.

Throughout the country, city addresses, school districts, and governing jurisdictions do not necessarily follow the same boundaries. You can't simply assume your address gives you all the information you need. What is true for school districts also stands true for services such as fire and police protection, trash pickup, water and sewage, utility hookups, and cable television. So, before you buy, make sure you verify the school district, property tax rates, and municipal services that will apply to your home to be.

Also, when you're talking to the secretary or clerk at the school district headquarters, the planning agency, or the tax assessor's office, be very specific about where you will live.

In Champaign, Illinois, Marlene Watts asked school personnel whether her home-to-be on Florida Street would put her kids in Wilson Junior High, which is the school she wanted. The secretary Marlene talked to replied yes. The correct answer was no. True, residents on the south side of Florida were within the Wilson Junior High school district. But homes on the north side of the street, where Marlene had moved, were not. Florida was the dividing line. It wasn't enough to live on Florida. You had to live on the south side of the street.

Remember Marlene's mistake: Verify municipal boundaries, school districts, taxes, and services as specifically as you can. As odd as it sounds, you may not live where you think you live.

Mistake No. 48:   *We didn't know there were stables nearby. The wind was blowing from a different direction the day we looked.*

Lesson: *Find out if any foul odors periodically intrude into the neighborhood.*

In the town where I was raised, relatively few homebuyers wanted to live in the southwest part of town. At least six or eight days a month a local chemical plant released huge volumes of what smelled like hydrogen sulfide (which smells worse than rotten eggs). This foul odor just hung in the air. Fortunately today, with much tougher environmental laws, industrial emissions don't cause quite the problem they used to. Still, not all noxious industrial odors have been eliminated. So if you are relocating to an area you don't know well, you might do some investigating.

However, industrial odors aren't all you need to think about. Kevin Conroy remembers the day he and his wife looked at the suburban development where they bought their lot to build a new home. "It was a crisp cool afternoon in early November," says Kevin. "We were looking forward to getting out of the city into the clean fresh country air. And that's what we found.

"Then one day during the following spring when we were pretty well along with our construction, we were almost knocked over by the strong odor of horse manure. We didn't know it at the time, but we soon found out. There were riding stables and a large horse farm less than a half-mile east of our development. Overall, we were lucky, I guess, because the wind doesn't come in from that direction very often. But when it does . . . "

Mistake No. 49:   *We didn't know we had bought in a flood plain.*

Lesson: *Ask your real estate agent or mortgage lender if your home is located in a flood plain. Then buy flood insurance.*

Every year throughout the United States, thousands of homeowners suffer heavy losses due to floods. All too frequently these losses could have been prevented. A case in point is Emily and Dennis Bruner.

Emily and Dennis bought their home in a flood plain. In and of itself, there's nothing unusual about that. Millions of American homes are located in flood plains. But (according to the Bruners), no one—not the previous homeowners (the sellers), the real estate agent, or their mortgage lender—explained to them the area's flood potential.

As a result, the Bruners didn't buy flood insurance. Sure enough, several years after Emily and Dennis bought their home, the Des Plaines River overran its banks. The torrent rushed through their home at depths of five feet or more. Their home's foundation was destroyed, as was its interior, all their furniture, and their personal belongings. Not counting the drowning of Emilé, their Yorkshire terrier, and the emotional trauma of losing their life's possessions, the Bruners' direct dollar losses totaled $60,000.

If this wasn't bad enough, their mortgage lender pushed the Bruners for full payment of their outstanding mortgage balance. The Bruners were without a home, without personal belongings, and saddled with a mortgage debt of $91,381. Bankruptcy looked like their only solution.

Eventually, when threatened with a lawsuit for failing to advise the Bruners to buy flood insurance, the mortgage lender backed off and forgave their debt. Still, even with debt forgiveness, the Bruners were out their direct losses and their accumulated home equity. They avoided bankruptcy, but the lack of flood insurance cost them their life's savings.

Flooding is a real risk that many homeowners face. Yet you can't adequately judge the flood potential of a neighborhood by driving through it. You need historical data. That's why the federal government has drawn up flood maps and designated certain areas as flood zones.

Of course, just because a home is located in a flood zone doesn't mean a flood is likely, or even imminent. In fact, some critics have complained the government has defined flood zones much too broadly. But would you rather be safe or sorry? To be safe, you should at least try to determine the danger of flooding. If it concerns you, then buy flood insurance. Your homeowners insurance policy will not pay for flood losses.

Mistake No. 50:   *After a downpour, you can't drive down these roads.*

Lesson: *Think bad weather. Will you be able to get to and from your home?*

If you're like most people, you will avoid looking at homes when it's raining so hard you'd have to hunch over the steering wheel to try to see where you're driving. Likewise, on those days ice and snow blanket the ground, you'd rather stretch out on the sofa, read a book, or watch a football game. For the great majority of homebuyers, bad weather is not the best time to shop for a home. Rather, the best time to look at houses is when the sun is shining, the days are nice, and you feel like getting out and driving around.

But think for a moment. On reasonably nice days, you won't be able to see whether snow or rain makes the roads leading to and from your home inaccessible. "We wanted to move out to the country so bad," says Stevie Rankin, "we didn't even consider what it would be like driving in during the winter snows or spring rains. But we found out. After a downpour or heavy snows, you can't drive down these roads. Sometimes it takes a couple of days for the snow plows to clear the roads. Then, if we're dumped on again, we're stuck for another couple of days.

"When it rains hard, the dirt road leading out to the county highway becomes so muddy, you can only use it as a last resort. We had to buy a four-wheel-drive Jeep Wagoneer."

Of course, dirt roads aren't the only potential source of trouble. More than a few cities and suburban developments have improperly graded streets and inadequate sewers for water runoff. I've seen neighborhoods where, after a heavy rain, the kids regularly get out and go "swimming" in the streets.

Also, in heavy rains, it's not uncommon for houses situated below grade to receive a flood of water flowing from the streets into their driveway, garage, or basement. (Remember, water does run downhill.) If you live where it sleets and snows, look at the grade of your driveway. Is it so steep you will have trouble pulling in or out of it?

Yes, go out and shop for your home on those nicer days. But at least think bad weather. When it's raining or snowing, will you be able to travel easily to and from your home?

Mistake No. 51:   *We hardly ever see the sun here.*

Lesson: *Discover your metro area's microclimates.*

Does your metro area have "microclimates"? In and around some cities, within commuting distance of a central business district, a July day might bring fog and 60 degree temperatures in one neighborhood, 70 degrees and rain in another, and 90 degrees and sunshine elsewhere. Oceans, lakes, rivers, hills, mountains, bays, and even tall buildings can affect weather patterns.

Within a 15-mile radius of downtown Vancouver, British Columbia, rainfall varies from 15 inches to more than 100 inches a year. In San Francisco, the Cow Hollow and Marina District neighborhoods enjoy noticeably less fog and more sunshine than other neighborhoods located near the zoo and the Pacific Ocean. If you live in Walnut Creek (20 minutes from the San Francisco Bay Bridge), you'll find many summer days over 80 degrees. To city residents, though, 80 degrees feels like a heat wave. In the Los Angeles metro area, hundreds of Ventura residents breathe (relatively) clean air, while in Palmdale residents suffer 150 smog-day warnings a year. Skyscraper office and apartment buildings not only block sunlight, they can dramatically affect wind velocity. (Don't try walking near the Sears Tower in Chicago or the World Trade Center in Manhattan on windy days.)

If you now live in a metro area with microclimates, you may know how weather differs among local neighborhoods and communities. On the other hand, if you are moving to a new area, talk to Realtors or perhaps call a government weather station. To avoid unwelcome surprises, it pays to know the weather patterns before you choose a neighborhood or location.

Mistake No. 52:   *We wanted to buy in the country to avoid the city's high property tax rates.*

Lesson: *Property taxes are only one side of the coin. Also compare government services.*

Many homebuyers flee the cities to locate in rural or suburban areas where they can find lower property tax rates. That's what motivated Jack Byers and his family. "We wanted to buy a home in the country," says Jack. "We knew once we moved outside the city limits, our tax rates would drop 30 percent. But I forgot about services. Out here in the country, we pay for our own trash collection; we are assessed separately by the fire district; and the city's water and sewage lines don't run out this far. That means we have to maintain a well and septic tank.

"We don't have gas lines either," Jack continued. "So our energy costs for drying clothes, home heating, water heating, and cooking are higher. Nor are we connected yet to cable television. And because the closest fire station is a partly volunteer outfit three miles away, we pay more for homeowners insurance than people in the city.

"I don't want to complain," Jack added. "I'm just saying, we didn't look at homes in the city because we wanted lower taxes. Now it looks like after we consider everything, living in the country's actually more expensive."

Sometimes it's easy to get so concerned about cutting taxes you forget cities do provide services. So when shopping locations, compare tax rates. But also compare what your taxes buy.

Mistake No. 53:   *After we bought, the city cut our services and raised our taxes.*

Lesson: *Determine whether your community is solvent.*

Everybody would like more services, better schools, and lower taxes. But many Americans are getting the opposite. Cities, counties, and states throughout the United States have fallen into a financial black hole. What we used to call financial irresponsibility now goes by the name revenue shortfall. But regardless of political semantics, the results are usually the same: higher taxes and cutbacks in education, libraries, street repairs, police protection, and social services. "The month after we moved in," says Shannon Brown, "they jacked up tax rates, canceled the bus service, and raised the tolls for the bridge."

If you're thinking about buying a home in a community that's running a large deficit—beware. Since state and local governments can't borrow with the same reckless abandon as the federal government, at some point—sooner rather than later—someone's got to pay the piper. And as likely as not, that someone will be the homeowners. Property tax rates will probably be headed up. You'll be paying more for less.

So before you buy, don't just look at current tax rates. Find out the financial condition of the community. Does it balance its books? Or is it headed toward insolvency like New York City?

As an added precaution, you might also ask your Realtor or the city treasurer's office about the level of the community's bonded indebtedness. Sometimes communities that expect rapid growth float bonds (borrow money) to pay for new streets, roads, sewage facilities, parks, libraries, schools, fire stations, and other types of infrastructure necessary to support housing development and an increasing population. (In California, these are called Mello Roos bonds). Over time the bonds will be paid off by taxing all the residents in the new developments. As long as growth occurs as expected, financing infrastructure this way generally doesn't create a problem.

However, if growth stalls or the local economy collapses, then early residents may end up with a serious problem. After the Colorado oil bust stalled growth in that state, for example, more than a few new developments and communities went bankrupt. Some owners of $100,000 houses were getting property tax bills for as much as $12,000 a year. Of course, most owners didn't pay these taxes. They just walked away from their houses. Lawyers for the tax authorities, mortgage lenders, and bond holders were left to litigate over the remains.

The Colorado experience was extreme. But it does illustrate an easily avoided mistake: Understand the risks of owning a home in a community that spends dangerously more than it takes in.

Mistake No. 54: *Everyone around here seems so apathetic. They've accepted decline.*

Lesson: Look for communities and neighborhoods with an entrepreneurial let-us-make-things-better spirit.

No law of the universe says a city, community, or neighborhood must decline. Or if down, it must stay down. Communities improve when they look at their strengths, search for ways to overcome problems, and develop a can-do attitude. They decline when people overlook their resources and advantages. As he watched the for-sale sign go up in his front yard, Paul Dillon says, "We didn't want to move, but everyone around here is so apathetic. They've accepted decline. We just don't want to be here as it happens."

More than 100 years ago, Henry Grady, editor of the *Atlanta Constitution*, put it like this as he used the funeral of a man to describe the dying of nearby Pickens County, Georgia:

> The grave was dug through solid marble, but the marble headstone came from Vermont. It was in a pine wilderness but the pine coffin came from Cincinnati. An iron mountain overshadowed it but the coffin nails and the screws and the shovel came from Pittsburgh. With hard wood and metal abounding, the corpse was hauled on a wagon from South Bend, Indiana. A hickory grove grew near by, but the pick and shovel handles came from New York. The cotton shirt on the dead man came from Cincinnati, the coat and breeches from Chicago, the shoes from Boston; the folded hands were encased in white gloves from New York, and round the poor neck, which had worn all its living days the bondage of lost opportunity, was twisted a cheap cravat from Philadelphia. Pickens County, so rich in undeveloped resources, furnished nothing for the funeral except the corpse and the hole in the ground and would probably have imported both of those if it could have done so. And as the poor dead fellow was lowered to his rest, on coffin bands from Lowell, he carried nothing into the next world as a reminder of his home in this, save the halted blood in his veins, the chilled marrow in his bones, and the echo of the dull clods that fell on his coffin lid.

The residents of Pickens County could not see their own opportunities and potential. Is this the type of community or neighborhood you're considering? Or is there an active entrepreneurial spirit that declares, "We can make things better. We can and will determine our own future." It was this spirit that lifted Pittsburgh, Denver, Austin, and Houston from their economic fall. It's this spirit that is bringing back neighborhoods like south-central Los Angeles, Candler Park (Atlanta), and Mt. Rainier (Washington, D.C.).

Mistake No. 55:   *The sellers said it was only 25 minutes to downtown by train.*

Lesson: *Planning to commute to work? Test travel the route before you buy.*

"True, it was only 25 minutes to downtown by train," recalls Andrew Ho. "But that was if you arrived at the platform on Saturday afternoon just as the train was about to pull out.

"On the other hand, if you're leaving our house to get to work by 9:00 A.M., you better be out the door by 7:30 at the latest. With the morning traffic backup at 95th, it can take 20 to 30 minutes just to get to the Sommerville station. Then parking (when you can find it) and walking to the platform takes another five to 10 minutes. And at commuter hours, the train takes 40 minutes, not 25. Next comes an eight-minute walk to the office. So that's about an hour and a half if everything goes without a hitch—which you can't always count on.

"We liked the house so much," Andrew adds, "I wanted to believe I could get to work in 30 to 40 minutes. I don't really blame the sellers for misleading me as much as I blame myself. Rather than discover the facts, I preferred to be blinded by illusion."

As Andrew now recognizes, when buying a home, it's easy to accept an illusion. You tell yourself what you want to believe. To avoid this mistake, test travel your commute during the hours you will be commuting. Whether driving or taking public transportation, you might find an assumed 30-minute trip actually puts you on the road for an hour and a half.

Mistake No. 56:   *We didn't walk the neighborhood.*

Lesson: *Walk and talk the streets where you plan to locate.*

Several months ago Carol and Omas Tabor bought their first home. It was located in a San Francisco neighborhood that looked pleasant enough when they discovered it on one of their weekend neighborhood excursions. But as the Tabors soon learned after they moved in, the neighborhood was infested with drug dealers. Even worse, a crack house was located just two doors down from their home. Shocked and hurt by what they now know, the Tabors are suing their real estate agent and the sellers of the property. The Tabors complain the agent and the former homeowners should have told them about the neighborhood drug problem.

Without prejudging the case, my inclination is that the Tabors are justified in their feelings. Yet to some degree they must share responsibility for this mistake. Before making an offer to buy their home, the Tabors should have walked the neighborhood and talked to the people who lived there—not just to get the facts on crime, but to discover other information that could help them decide whether they wanted to live there. For example:

- Are the residents friendly? Do they welcome newcomers, or are they stand-offish?
- Where are most people in the neighborhood employed? What are their occupations? Are their jobs and employers solid or unstable?
- Are there any recent or planned zoning changes? Street widenings? Commercial or apartment construction?
- Do the streets flood when it rains hard? Are the streets cleared promptly after a snowfall?
- Is the neighborhood plagued with noisy neighbors or other disturbances?
- What types of people are moving in and moving out of the neighborhood? Is it heading upscale, downscale, or holding its own?
- Is there an action-oriented homeowners association that's working to improve the neighborhood?
- If residents could change three things in the neighborhood, what would they list?
- Do residents think they receive good public services for the taxes they pay?
- What schools do neighborhood children attend? What are their strengths and weaknesses? Who's doing what to improve them?

In addition to talking with residents, walking the neighborhood can help you sharpen and focus your observations.

- Look closely at the houses. Do they show signs of neglect and disrepair? Or do nearly all people show pride in their properties?
- Are the yards well landscaped? Have residents accented their homes with flowers, shrubs, and other attractive plantings?
- Do you hear any disturbances or detect unpleasant odors?

- Are the parks and public spaces well kept? Or are they littered with sacks from McDonald's, marred by graffiti, and populated by derelicts?

- Do any (or many) of the houses show multiple mailboxes or cars stacked up in driveways?

- Do you see signs of home remodeling, improvements, or renovation?

Your real estate agent and the sellers *should tell* you about the neighborhood. But you can learn even more by *experiencing* it for yourself.

Chapter 5

Comparing Homes

Mistake No. 57: *My agent told me this was a good school district.*

Lesson: *Never accept a real estate agent's subjective comments at face value. Concentrate on verifiable facts.*

"When I started looking for a home," says Lori Pines, "I wanted the Richmond neighborhood. My sister has two kids over there in Jefferson Elementary, and she thinks it's great. Since my two are age four and six, a good elementary school was very important to me. Besides, it would have been nice to live near Sandy and Rick.

"But the problem was I really couldn't find a house I liked at a price I wanted to pay. So my agent suggested I look in Brookview. She said I could get more house for the money and that the schools there were just as good as Richmond's.

"Well, the agent was right about one thing. I found a house I loved in Brookview for about $25,000 less than it would have cost in Richmond. But I got so excited about the house, I forgot to check out the schools.

"I just accepted my agent's comments at face value. Boy, what a mistake that was. I'm now having to drive Lisa and Sean halfway across town every morning to a private school. The money I saved on the house I'm spending for gas and tuition."

Did Lori's agent really mislead her about the quality of the schools in Brookview? Maybe. Maybe not. Could Lori have easily avoided her mistake? Definitely yes. Lori should have followed this rule: Don't ask your real estate agent for opinions. Ask for facts. Then verify.

When working with an agent—especially an agent with whom you've developed rapport—it's easy to rapid-fire questions: "Is this a good neighborhood? Is there much crime in this area? Is that house overpriced? Is the house in good condition? How long does it take to get to downtown from here? Is this a good school district?

Now think for a moment about these questions. What is a "good" neighborhood, school district, or property condition? What is "too much" crime? What does "overpriced" mean? Overpriced relative to what? Going downtown? By what route? To which building? At what time of the day? For answers you can rely on, you need to ask more concrete questions. And you need to push your real estate agent to answer with facts.

Telling you the commute to downtown is a "breeze" doesn't give quite the same information as: "Between 7:30 and 9:00 A.M., the commute will normally range between 25 and 35 minutes." To an executive used to a 6:00 A.M., 90-minute drive from Long Island to Manhattan, a 25- to 35-minute commute might easily qualify as a "breeze." To an Indiana University professor who can walk to her office in less than 10 minutes, a 25- to 35-minute hassle with traffic everyday could bring on ulcers.

As to crime, consider a divorced mother with two children. She's in residency at a hospital. She'll be working long hours at all times of night and day. She plans to ride her bike to work. Compare her likely definition of "too much" crime to a 34-year-old single man who is 6'4," a triathlete, and an ex-Golden Gloves boxer. "Let 'em try something with me" might be his attitude.

By asking your agent for facts, not opinions, you'll significantly reduce the chance the two of you are talking on different wavelengths. Remember, career real estate agents want to do the best job they can for their homebuyers and sellers. To earn a living, they need repeat business and referrals from satisfied clients. You can help them help you by asking concrete questions they can answer with verifiable facts. "The mean SAT score of college-bound seniors last year at Lincoln High was 1150," tells you much more than "I believe Lincoln High enjoys a very good reputation." Knowing there were 27 house break-ins in the neighborhood during the past six months tells you much more than the subjective report, "This is a relatively safe neighborhood."

All of these opinion statements may be "true." But the factual statements convey more useful information and leave less room for a "difference of opinion."

Mistake No. 58:   *Our agent was part order taker, part chauffeur, and part narrator—but she didn't really give us the service we needed.*

Lesson: *Know what services you expect from your agent, then work with an agent who delivers.*

"Since this was our first home," Peter Chen reflects, "we didn't really know what to expect from a real estate agent. Ours was friendly enough. But she hardly did anything that we couldn't have done for ourselves. She seemed like she just wanted to take our order, chauffeur us around, and then act as a narrator or announcer.

"She'd say things like 'What kind of home are you looking for? What neighborhood do you want? What price range fits your budget?'

"The problem," says Peter, "is that we weren't sure what, where, or how much. That seemed to frustrate her. When she did drive us around to look at houses, she didn't seem to know very much. Once inside a house, her major contribution to helping us evaluate the house was 'This is the living room. This is the kitchen. This is the master bedroom.' Even with us being first-timers, we know a kitchen when we see one.

"But as I said," Peter continued, "she was nice, so we didn't want to hurt her feelings and switch agents. In the end, though, we realized we made a mistake by sticking with her. I think with a better agent we could have explored more options and made a better choice. In fact, after it was over, we laughed because we realized how silly it was for us to stick with an agent we certainly would not recommend to our friends."

Peter Chen and his wife fell into the same trap that catches many first-time homebuyers. They called a real estate office about a listing, got hooked up with an agent who wanted to show them some houses, and then stayed with the agent (more or less) by default. You can prevent this mistake by learning what service to expect from an agent and then working only with an agent who delivers.

Although not all homebuyers need the same services, here are many of the ways a real estate professional should be willing and able to help you make a better home-buying decision.

- Talk through your housing wants and needs. Help you clarify and rank your priorities.

- Go over your finances, help you improve your "borrower profile," and suggest finance plans and lenders that can maximize your affordability.

- Suggest trade-offs and compromises that will help you satisfy your most critical needs and priorities.

- Inform you about neighborhoods, communities, and developments that seem right for you.

- Provide you market facts, such as recent sales prices and time-on-the-market data for homes similar to the ones you're interested in.

- Alert you to good buys as soon as (sometimes even before) they come on the market.

- Get the sellers of homes you're interested in to prepare a "Seller Disclosures Statement." A disclosure statement should warn you of deficiencies or defects that can mar the desirability of a home or its neighborhood.

- Point out ways you might improve (redecorate, remodel, renovate) a home to enhance its market value or better meet the needs of your family (preferably both).

- Stay in tune with your home-buying efforts from beginning to end. Make sure everything gets taken care of that needs to be taken care of.

- Anticipate, prevent, or overcome roadblocks or problems that may arise. Keep you fully informed. Pave the way for as smooth and successful home-buying experience as possible.

You may not want or need all of these services mentioned here. But you do require more service than order taker, chauffeur, and narrator. Successful real estate agents have worked with dozens (often hundreds) of homebuyers. They've run up against all types of homebuyer problems, obstacles, and goals. By expecting and requiring agents to deliver a variety of services, you gain the benefit of their expertise, insight, and experience. Remember: The best real estate professionals don't *sell* real estate. They help people become homeowners by helping to solve problems.

Mistake No. 59:   *Our agent never mentioned . . .*

Lesson: *Always ask sales agents (or sellers) for specific factual disclosures that list the defects or problems of a home and its neighborhood.*

One of the most misunderstood topics in real estate is the legal concept of "disclosure." Because the laws and practices of disclosure are constantly changing, many home sellers, buyers, and even sales agents have become confused.

From the early 1900s up to the 1960s, real estate agents represented sellers. Legally, agents were required to work exclusively for the interests of the property owners. In contrast, with respect to homebuyers, the rule was *caveat emptor*, "let the buyer beware." In most home purchases, the law neither required sellers nor their agents to reveal a home's defects. If you didn't discover a home's crumbling foundation or inadequate wiring until after you bought it, that was your tough luck. You had little recourse to the sellers and even less to the agent. Unless the sellers or their agent gave explicitly false warranties or representations—"That foundation could support a 12-story building"—you were assumed to have bought the home in as-is condition.

Today, however, the doctrine of *caveat emptor* is dead. From the late 1960s and still evolving up through the present, innumerable court decisions, federal and state laws and regulations, and real estate licensing standards have sealed the coffin lid on "let the buyer beware." The general rule has become "let the sellers and their agents beware." The consumer is king.

What all this means is that today the law gives little comfort to sellers or agents who fail to disclose a property's serious defects. Regardless of whether you're working with a "seller's" agent, a "buyer's" agent, or a "dual" agent, any agent who doesn't mention a property's serious defects can be held liable for that omission. Yet everything is not as clear cut as it seems. And here's where mistakes are made.

SERIOUS DEFECTS

First, what kinds of defects qualify as "serious"? At one extreme is a recent Massachusetts case. A house had a dangerously defective gas heater. On several occasions the heater had malfunctioned. The soon-to-be seller was told by the repairman the heater could easily malfunction again and start a fire. Even with this warning, though, the seller did not replace or adequately repair the heater. Nor did he inform the eventual buyers of the home.

Shortly after the buyers took possession, the heater exploded. This time the results were fatal. Two members of the family died. The court held the seller criminally liable. He was convicted of involuntary manslaughter and sentenced to 15 years in prison.

Defects in a home that could likely lead to extensive property damage, injury, or death are serious. Both sellers and agents must disclose them or suffer the consequences. But what about substandard wiring that is in good condition and has never created a problem? That's a gray area. What about several light switches and electrical outlets that don't work? Those are probably not serious.

It is because of these gray areas of liability and uncertainties—not to mention potential injury or loss of life—that you must explicitly insist that sellers and agents list all of a home's problems. Many sellers, and some agents, have not adjusted to the demise of caveat emptor.

To illustrate: Consider this question of a would-be seller. In a recent letter to Q&A columnist Nina Groskind (*Boston Globe*, April 25, 1993, p. A6), this homeowner writes that he knows his home has "several flaws, some minor, some more significant." He then asks (evidently fully prepared to hide as much as possible), "What obligation do I have to 'tell all' to people interested in purchasing my home?"

Ms. Groskind answers that the homeowner might be able to get away with "nondisclosure." But (1) he'd better not tell his real estate agent, because the agent would have to pass the information along to the buyer; and (2) the owner should not make any explicit false statement that could mislead any prospective new owners of the home. It's sellers like these that you must guard against.

"KNOWN" OR "SUSPECTED" DEFECTS

As you try to get as much information as you can about a prospective home and neighborhood, another type of problem arises. What if the seller or the agent doesn't know about the termites in the foundation or the wood rot under the roof shingles? What if they don't "know" but only "suspect" a defect might exist? In the case of no knowledge, courts generally rule that sellers or agents can't be expected to disclose what they don't know. However, ignorance doesn't offer an airtight defense.

Laws in many states require owners or agents to make certain kinds of property investigations. In Massachusetts sellers must test their homes for urea formaldehyde foam insulation. In California real estate agents must visually inspect most homes they list for sale. Even further, some judges and juries have held sellers or agents liable for not disclosing defects they should have known about or reasonably suspected might exist—even though they claimed no direct knowledge.

In a far-reaching California case in 1986, a realty firm was held liable for not "disclosing" that a home's hillside location made it susceptible to damage from mudslides. The agent claimed no knowledge or expertise on the topic of mudslides. The court said "too bad." Even if the agent didn't know, he should have reasonably suspected there might be a problem.

As you can now see, the entire area of inspections and disclosures can confuse everyone involved in a home-buying transaction. In so many ways the "law" is ambiguous or simply not well understood. That's why the entire area of "disclosure" and "nondisclosure" contributes to so many home-buying mistakes. Of course, the traditional tendency and practice of sellers to hide or understate defects adds to the potential for error. But there's also another longstanding practice and tradition in home buying that can divert you from getting the information you need to make a good decision. It's call "puffery."

BEWARE OF PUFFERY

"This is a great neighborhood. You're really getting a bargain. This home's in superb condition. You'll just love the people here. Oh yes, it's very quiet." Often homebuyers who don't get the information they need fail because they unconsciously accept puffery in lieu of facts. (See Mistake No. 57.) None of these statements actually includes any factual information.

Some unethical agents (or sellers), though, purposely use puffery to mask their lack of knowledge or as an explicit attempt to avoid disclosure. These agents have learned to couch their comments in terms of puffery or "debatable" opinions because opinions permit them to escape liability for misleading you.

"You said this was a great neighborhood," complain the angry homebuyers to the agent who sold them their home.

"Well, it is a great neighborhood," responds the agent. "Sure there's a crack house several doors down and I know the drive-by shootings can be annoying. But the neighborhood association is working hard to turn things around. All this community spirit really does make this a great neighborhood. You just can't find that spirit and feeling of togetherness in many neighborhoods these days."

By the agent's definition, the neighborhood is a "great" one. Can you prove your definition of "great" should outweigh the agent's? Did the agent misrepresent the neighborhood? Or were his comments merely sales puffery and a matter of opinion? If you took a case like this to court, you would probably stand a better chance of winning today than in years past. But in most states you'd still be better off spending your money on lottery tickets rather than on lawyers.

EXCEPTIONS TO THE LAWS OF DISCLOSURE

Although society is generally moving away from the doctrine of *caveat emptor*, the evolving laws still exclude some types of sellers, properties, and transactions. For example, government agencies, financial institutions, auctioneers, and court-appointed trustees may not be covered under some disclosure laws. Buyers of commercial and investment real estate receive less protection than homebuyers. And if you're thinking of buying at a foreclosure sale or through probate, you will probably be buying "as is." Also, in some states, FSBOs (owners who sell their homes without an agent) need not meet the same high standards of disclosure required of real estate agents.

RULES TO FOLLOW

When you shop for a home, you want to get the best information you can. In general, today's laws of disclosure make this job somewhat easier than it's been in the past. Yet disclosure laws aren't the full answer to the difficult task of information gathering. They scatter into many gray areas; they may be circumvented by puffery; they may not be understood adequately by agents or sellers; and these laws frequently carve out exceptions for certain types of persons, properties, or transactions.

As a result, your home-buying efforts must be proactive. To prevent mistakes, you can't simply depend on others to reveal all they know or should know about a home and its neighborhood. Take the initiative to protect yourself by following these rules.

- Ask your real estate agent (or lawyer) to explain fully the laws of disclosure that apply to home buying in your area. Learn where disclosure laws may not apply; learn the types of nondisclosure problems that are prone to arise in the homes or neighborhoods you're looking at.

- Always ask your agent specific questions that require factual answers. Don't settle for "debatable" opinions without further probing.

- Ask the sellers to prepare a written list of every defect, problem, or shortcoming of their home and neighborhood. If something's not 100 percent right, tell them you want to know about it.

- Don't casually accept agent or seller evasions such as , "I believe," "I think," or "as far as we know." If the sellers or their agent don't truly know, then make a note to follow-up with further inquiry or investigation. Too many homebuyers mistakenly accept these kinds of seller or agent "hedges."

- Hire professional inspectors to critically examine the condition of the house, its component systems (heating, air conditioning, electrical, ventilation), and built-in appliances.

- Closely inspect the home and neighborhood yourself. In the final analysis, it's going to be your house. The most successful homebuyers take charge of the inspection process.

- Assume everyone you're working with is acting in good faith. But take precautions as if they weren't.

Mistake No. 60:   *We didn't need to hire a professional inspector. My dad knows all about houses.*

Lesson: *You might ask your dad, brother-in-law, or Uncle Harry to inspect your home as an additional safeguard. But don't substitute family members or friends for a professional inspection.*

If a friend or family member "knows all about houses," you may be tempted to skip a professional inspection and save yourself $200 or $300. Don't do it. Marci Alvarez tells why.

"When we bought, we were short of cash. So I asked my dad to inspect our house for us. He has worked as a painter, a carpenter, and even built a den and an extra bath for my parents' house. With all that experience, I figured he would be able to discover any trouble spots. Unfortunately for all of us, he missed some type of problem with the fuse box and the wiring. After we moved in, we must have blown a dozen fuses, and several wall outlets kept getting real hot everytime we plugged something in and turned it on.

"When I told my dad about the problem, he tried to fix it, but I think he just made it worse. Eventually, we did get an electrician out to the house. By the time he finished his rewiring, his bill went over $900.

"If that wasn't bad enough, my husband first blamed me and next blamed my dad. They argued over it for several weeks. Let me tell you, it was not fun. Spending $900 for circuit breakers and whatever else it was the electrician charged us for was bad enough. But the family turmoil was even worse.

"Then after I thought the whole episode was behind us, my dad insisted on giving us a check for $900. We didn't want it. But there was no way we could refuse without more arguing. So now we have the $900, but I feel guilty about accepting the money and regret ever getting my dad involved in the first place."

When it comes time to get your home inspected, hire a professional house inspector. Professional inspectors evaluate dozens of houses a month. They know what to look for. They own the necessary tools of their trade. They learn to recognize signs of problems in their early stages so they can caution you about what to expect in the future. Moreover, professional home inspectors take on financial liability for any mistakes they do make.

Ask your family and friends to join with you to celebrate the joy and achievement of your becoming a homeowner. Don't ask them to shoulder the full responsibilities of inspecting a home. If tempted, remember Marci's experience.

Mistake No. 61:   *We didn't think a new home needed to be professionally inspected.*

Lesson: *Even when you're 100 percent sure of your builder's reputation, buy a little extra peace of mind and secure a professional inspection.*

"Christine Estep is weary—weary of paying for a home she can't live in," opened a recent front-page article in the *Miami Herald* (May 2, 1993). Christine Estep is one of the tens of thousands of homeowners whose homes were damaged by Hurricane Andrew. But instead of having her home repaired, Christine and the other 343 homeowners in her Village Homes condominium complex are about to see their homes demolished. The relatively new complex was "so riddled with construction defects" that engineers have recommended tearing down all the units and rebuilding from scratch.

To make matters worse, the developer of the complex was the well-known Florida development company, Arvida. And at the time of the first phase of construction, Arvida was a subsidiary of the Walt Disney Company. After Disney, another company of high standing, JMB Realty of Chicago, became Arvida's parent. Although in a multimillion-dollar case like this, charges and countercharges fly about among homeowners, architects, lawyers, engineers, and contractors, no one seems to dispute the homeowners engineers' basic conclusion that the construction quality of the homes in the Village Homes complex failed to meet even minimum standards of safety.

Engineers, as well as a government investigators, say the homes had undersized foundations, inadequately designed roof trusses, masonry walls without the necessary steel reinforcement, unanchored support posts, and missing hurricane straps. Now you might wonder, aren't newly constructed homes supposed to be inspected and approved by government building inspectors? How could major defects slip by? A lot of other people are asking the same questions. But it's not the first time.

Over the years most cities throughout the United States have been rocked by various types of permits-for-sale bribery and payoff scandals. In fact, in 1990 Janet Reno, now attorney general of the United States, was the Florida State's attorney for Dade County (Miami). In that capacity, she spearheaded a drive to investigate the building inspection process. Ms. Reno never charged anyone with a crime, but her office investigation did result in charges of lax enforcement of building codes.

One building inspector who was followed by an investigator, for example, managed to inspect and permit seven homes in five minutes. A former building inspector in Dade was quoted by the *Miami Herald* as saying "It was a farce. The building and zoning department for years pushed quantity, not quality."

My purpose here is not to point the finger at anybody. It will be years (if ever) before a complete accounting of errors and responsibilities are tallied up and assigned to the various parties involved in Christine Estep's case. But you should know the construction defects and lax inspection practices that contributed to Christine's emotional and financial worries are all too common. Just because a home is new (or nearly new) does not mean it's defect free. A few builders and developers are crooks; others are careless; some need to cut corners "temporarily" to stay solvent; and others just plain make mistakes. Any way you look at it, new does not necessarily mean perfect.

Avoid unpleasant surprises. Employ a professional inspector even when you're buying a new or recently built house or condominium.

Mistake No. 62:   *I thought lead paint had been outlawed years ago.*

Lesson: Environmental concerns have come home.

When your concerns turn to the environment, you may think of disappearing habitat for the spotted owls, mass illegal killings of elephants for their ivory tusks, or perhaps clear-cutting the African and Amazonian rain forests. But some of the most dangerous environmental problems may actually lie right where you live.

Jackie Shattuck and her husband, Mike, recently bought a home. Their inspection report showed the house to be nearly defect free. The wiring, plumbing, roof, foundation, and appliances were all found to be in good condition. Unhappily, however, the Shattucks thought only of the physical condition of their home. They forgot to check its environmental quality. That mistake cost them nearly $5,000.

"Lead paint," Jackie recalls saying when she heard the bad news. "I thought it had been outlawed years ago."

As a matter of law, Jackie was right. Once it was learned that lead-based paints could cause serious illnesses including brain damage (especially to children), this toxic metal was phased out of use in household paints. Prior to 1977, though, lead was a common ingredient. Although no one knows exactly how many older homes still have layers of lead-based paint lurking under less toxic (and more recent) paintings, estimates place the number somewhere between 20 and 40 million houses. "If you're buying a home built before the late 1970s," advises lead specialist Stephanie Pollack, "assume there's lead until proven otherwise."

To remove the danger of lead-based paint (which is called deleading) requires trained specialists with special equipment and protective gear. Depending on the size of the house and the number of rooms affected, deleading a home can easily cost $3,500 and may run up to $6,000 or more. Without deleading, paint chipping and flaking through natural wear can create a health hazard. Should you begin sanding, tearing out walls, or other particle-disturbing remodeling efforts, lead-based paint becomes a clear and present danger. Inhaling lead paint dust can cause permanent respiratory or neurological damage.

Of course, lead-based paint isn't the only potential contaminate homebuyers need to have checked before they buy. San Francisco Board of Supervisors member Angela Alioto, an outspoken environmentalist, recently discovered an old, long-out-of-use buried oil tank in her home's yard. To remove the tank and clean up the soil cost Ms. Alioto $9,000. When journalists questioned the councilwoman, she admitted she had not had her home inspected for environmental dangers before she bought it.

Don't make this same mistake. Environmental dangers can threaten health and sometimes cost thousands of dollars to remedy. This is one instance where "better safe than sorry" really applies. The exact type of environmental dangers you might confront will vary by where you live, the age of the home you're planning to buy, and the type of building practices and materials used in your area.

Your best bet is to talk with local or state environmental agencies. Many of these agencies have published environmental booklets that are written especially for homebuyers and homeowners. You might also be able to pick up an environmental booklet from your local Realtor. After investigation, you may decide against a full comprehensive environmental inspection of your home-to-be. But stay alert for at least the following types of potential problems.

• Lead-based paint

- Lead pipes or lead solder
- Asbestos (commonly found in many types of building supplies, materials, and floor tiles)
- Formaldehyde, especially urea formaldehyde foam insulation
- Contaminated ground water
- Volatile organic compounds (VOCs are found in most household chemicals, adhesives used with wall-to-wall carpeting, and pesticides)
- Radon (a gas released by radioactive decay that rises up from the ground especially into the lower levels of a home)
- Underground heating oil tanks
- High-power electrical lines and transformers

In our industrial world, no one can escape all pollution and contaminants. Still, you should at least try to identify risks, assess their relative dangers, and estimate the cost of cleanup. The environmental quality of a home ranks just as important as the condition of its roof or foundation.

Mistake No. 63: *Now we know why the sellers recently put up paneling in the downstairs den.*

Lesson: *Be cautious of recent redecorating, repairs, or remodeling by sellers. They may be hiding a problem.*

"If you want to get top dollar for your house when you sell, put it in tiptop condition." Over the years, this frequent advice from books and real estate agents has encouraged millions of homeowners to clean up, paint, wallpaper, panel, or otherwise redecorate and repair their homes before they place them on the market. "Package your home for profit," writes Peter Percelay in his book by the same title. "By effectively packaging your home, rather than just putting it on the market, you can reap thousands of additional dollars on your sale."

Percelay then goes on to tell his readers, "Your goal is to give buyers confidence in your product. . . . But you should never use packaging techniques as a way of hiding serious problems or defects in your home." Yes, and you should never inflate your resume, pad your expense account, or bring pens, pencils, and Scotch tape home from the office. But some people do.

Within our society, there are dishonest practices that, even if not widely accepted, are at least widely practiced. Hiding a home's defects through redecorating or remodeling seems to be one of them.

When you're shopping for a home, stay alert to this possibility. Many people who consider themselves honest have nevertheless imbibed too much of the spirit of *caveat emptor*. More than 200 years of this attitude and approach to sales hasn't been eradicated by two decades of consumerism. Sally Roth knows from experience.

Sally bought a home that was built into a hillside and had a lower-level den. Not long before the sellers had put their home up for sale, they had "packaged it for profit" by installing wood paneling on the walls of the den. Not only did the paneling add a nice aesthetic touch, it perfectly hid the permanent waterstain marks that showed where water poured through during the rainy season. Since Sally moved into the home in July, she didn't learn of the problem until the wet months of November and December.

Most people who prepare a home for sale do simply want to enhance its appeal. They're not trying to hide anything. But some people are. So if you find a home you're looking at has been freshly painted, plastered, paneled, wallpapered, repaired, or redecorated, closely inspect the improvements. As diplomatically as you can, secure written disclosures and warranties that pertain specifically to the condition of the property before the improvements were made. As I said before, assume the sellers are honest, but inspect the home as if they weren't.

Mistake No. 64: *After we moved in, the sellers' remodeling contractor put a lien against our home. And we had to pay it!*

Lesson: *Ask to see the sellers' receipts to verify that all recent work on the home has been paid in full.*

Every state in the country allows contractors and suppliers to place a lien against a home for unpaid work or materials. The exact nature of the laws differ, but generally they give firms and tradesmen at least 90 and sometimes up to 180 days after they have completed their work to file a lien.

In Rob Shoo's case, his sellers had remodeled a back porch into a sunroom at a cost of $2,700. The work was completed in late February.

In March the sellers placed the house up for sale. In early April Rob put in his contract and the owners accepted. The transaction closed in mid-May. On May 27 the Dependable Construction Company filed a mechanic's lien for unpaid wages and materials.

As a matter of law, the sellers were financially liable for the charges. But the mechanic's lien establishes a valid claim by Dependable Construction against the house—regardless of who now owns it. The lien sits in the public records as a cloud on the home's title. Unless Rob can somehow get the sellers to write a check for the amounts they owe, at some point he will have to write a check himself. As long as the mechanic's lien remains unpaid, Rob cannot sell or refinance his home.

To avoid this potential mistake, make sure you check the sellers' receipts for any work that has been performed recently on the house. As a further precaution, in some areas it's common to ask sellers to sign an affidavit stating: (1) All work performed has been paid in full; or (2) no work to the home has been performed within the past 90 days (or whatever other statute of limitation for filing liens applies). Should you buy a home with recent improvements, don't just assume the contractors have been paid. If you do, you run the risk of paying for them twice—once when you buy the home, once again when you need to pay the mechanic's lien to clear the home's title.

Mistake No. 65: *We should have looked at the sellers' utility bills.*

Lesson: *Energy audit a home before you buy it.*

"We were renting a house just about the same size as the one we bought," says Patty Snyder, "so we thought we had a pretty good fix on how much our utility bills would run in our new home. Boy, were we mistaken! Believe it or not, our heat and air-conditioning bills nearly doubled. Our PG&E is now averaging $230 a month. We should have examined the sellers' utility bills."

As most energy rates have stabilized somewhat since their big run-up in the 1970s, many homebuyers have forgotten that the total utility costs of operating a household can amount to $3,000 to $5,000 a year. With utility bills at these levels, an energy-efficient house can easily save you $750 to $2,000 a year—or even more. I've talked with some homeowners in Maine and Vermont who, with energy-oriented improvements, have even managed to cut their *total* winter heating bill to as low as $900 a year.

One simple way to check a home's utility consumption is to examine the sellers' utility bills. That won't tell you everything you need to know because you'll have to adjust for their family size, lifestyle, and heating and cooling comfort zones. But if you find their winter heating or summer cooling bills top say $300 or $400 a month, you may want to find out why.

Besides looking at utility bills, examine the windows, doors, appliances, water heater, furnace, and air conditioner. Do these promote energy consumption or conservation? What about the site placement and exterior design of the house? Is the home situated to protect against north winter winds as it brings in sunlight from the south? What about water usage? Fresh water for household consumption is becoming a more expensive resource. Does the yard require heavy watering? Are the showers and toilets equipped with water-saving devices? What's the political climate? Is it likely your local or state government will require an "energy retrofit" for the home at some time in the future?

In many parts of the country, utility costs rank right after mortgage payments as the second largest household cost—higher than property insurance, maintenance, or property taxes. Since energy-efficient houses can bring you savings of thousands of dollars, don't mistakenly leave this factor out when you're comparing different homes.

Mistake No. 66:   *We underestimated how much all of those little repairs and renovations could add up to.*

Lesson: Little things can mean a lot.

If you buy an existing home, you probably won't be able to find one that perfectly suits your needs or fits your tastes. More than likely you'll want to do some painting and wallpapering, lay new carpeting, repair the wood rot around the eves, enclose a porch, put in a skylight or two, restore the hardwood floors, strip the white paint and refurbish those natural oak doors and moldings, patch the roof, and maybe remodel a bath and kitchen.

How much money, time, and effort will all these little repairs and renovations add up to? Make a guess. Double it. Then add a 50 percent contingency factor. You may then come close to a reasonable answer. There seems to be some unwritten law of the universe that everything can be expected to cost more and take longer than you originally think. This is clearly true of putting a house into the shape you'd like.

From my experience, I would compare it to paying bills. You sit down to write a few checks for $50, $100, maybe $200, and all of a sudden, the checking account balance drops $1,800. How do all those little checks add up to such a large amount? I don't know, but they sure do.

Anyway, when you evaluate a home, don't forget little things do add up. After you've thought about all the individual repairs, redecorating, and renovation you'd like to do, write out a list. Make it as comprehensive as possible. Check the figures with qualified contractors or suppliers. Most important, don't simply keep a bunch of little numbers running around in your head. Total them.

Through redecorating and renovation you can boost your home's value by thousands of dollars. But whether these thousands actually turn up as profit or loss depends on how well you anticipate and budget your costs.

Mistake No. 67: *Before we could add central heat and air, we had to spend $1,800 for new wiring and ductwork.*

Lesson: *Often, planned repairs and renovations can't be made without incurring some other unplanned costs.*

You may find out a new roof costs $3,500. But if the sheets of plywood under the shingles that have been leaking have suffered wood rot (water plus wood equals rotten wood), your costs could climb to $4,500 or more. If interior ceilings and supports also have been water-damaged, the costs could go higher.

When Doc and Carrie Sheth bought their Galveston, Texas, home, they planned to spend $2,800 to add central heat and air conditioning. Their actual bill came to over $4,600. Although Doc and Carrie figured right about the cost of the heat and air unit they wanted, they forgot to add in the costs of upgrading their 100 amp electrical system to 200 amps. The upgrade was necessary to power their heat and AC system safely. Also, since the previous heating units in the house had been gas floor heaters, their home lacked ductwork, outlets, and air returns. These things further pushed up their costs.

Often, planned repairs and renovations will cost more than you originally figure because the work you want can't be performed by itself. To do this, you must first do that. Or we might say, in home repair and renovation, one thing often leads to another.

Unfortunately, many contractors calculate their estimates only for the basic work. Some purposely lowball their bids to get you committed to the job. Then they "discover" other work that must (or should) be performed. In other instances, it really is impossible to know the full extent of necessary repairs until well into the work. For example, all competent heating and air-conditioning contractors know the necessary electrical upgrade their heat and air units will require. However, roofing contractors may not know how much wood damage a house has suffered until they rip off the old roof.

No perfect way exists to handle this problem. But you can try to get a "no-surprises" estimate. Also, as a matter of good communication, make sure your contractor (or other cost estimator) understands you want to know the costs (or at least the nature) of all the labor and materials necessary to finish off your total repair or renovation. You also could ask for a worst-case/best-case range of estimates. At least then you could see a lower and an upper limit. None of these solutions is perfect because even the best plans and "no-surprise" estimates can miss the mark. (The construction budget for the world-famous Sydney, Australia, Opera House began at $6 million. Total costs at completion were over $100 million.)

The main issue, though, is to recognize that many types of repairs and renovations will require additional, and often unanticipated, expenses. So if you plan to buy a home that needs work, keep the risk of cost overruns in mind. Use this fact to help negotiate a lower price. You can reduce this risk through good planning and communication, but it's a mistake to think you can eliminate it entirely.

Mistake No. 68:   *The house looked great. I just didn't like cold showers, my son's favorite radio station, or lugging groceries up the stairs from the garage.*

Lesson: Looks aren't everything. Evaluate a home's livability as closely as you do its appearance and condition.

The feeling's great when you first see a house you fall in love with. High ceilings, hardwood floors, lots of natural light, a large country kitchen, a big stone fireplace, beautifully finished woodwork: The house could work as a photo feature for *Architectural Digest*. Before you jump to make an offer, though, evaluate whether the house could work for you. Don't mistake great looks for livability.

As a start, walk the floor plan—not for the purpose of viewing the rooms, but to judge accessibility and convenience. In your use of the house, what rooms will require frequent travel between them? How many steps is it from the master bedroom to the kitchen, the laundry facilities, or the main living area? How convenient is the parking (garage, carport, street) to the kitchen? Imagine yourself carrying several bags of groceries from your car to the kitchen.

Now enter the kitchen. Ideally, you should be able to work efficiently between the stove (oven), the sink, and the refrigerator. This area is called the work triangle. A poorly designed work triangle can add substantial time and hundreds of steps a day to food preparation and cleanup. Next measure the kitchen counter space, cabinet space, and location. Are cabinets and counters situated to provide enough room to work, prepare, and store food and kitchen supplies conveniently?

Upon leaving the kitchen, turn on the dishwasher. How loud is it? Can you hear it in other parts of the house? What about your television, radios, and stereos? Where will you place them? Take a portable radio from room to room. Can you play it without hearing the sounds elsewhere in the house? Problems with noise rankle many homeowners and family members. Do you really want to hear heavy metal blasting from your son's bedroom at 10:00 o'clock at night?

What about privacy? Does the floor plan of the home provide enough private space? Can you get away from each other if you want to?

Next check the bathrooms. How convenient are they? How long must the water run before you get hot water? How strong is the water pressure in the showers? Does the pressure ebb when someone flushes a toilet or turns on a faucet or another shower elsewhere? Does the water temperature hold constant? Can you hear a running shower or flushing toilet throughout the house? Do the bathrooms have enough natural or artificial light?

Once you've completed a livability inspection of a home's interior, go outside. Admire the azaleas, the hedges, the flowers, the expansive yard. Now think negatively. How much care will all this greenery require? Do you want to spend your weekends pulling weeds, trimming bushes, and cutting grass? Can you afford to pay someone else to do it for you? Cast your eyes around the exterior of the home. How much time and money must you spend to maintain the appearance and condition of the home properly?

Winding up your exterior inspection, go to the main entrance. Must future visitors stand in the rain until you let them in? Or is there an adequate area that protects from the weather? Step back inside the house; is there a nearby coat closet? Imagining the way you will live in the house, what would incoming visitors see: Piled-up dirty dishes in the kitchen? Children's toys scattered about? A pristine formal reception area and living room?

Next, turn away from the perspective of your visitors. Think about the house as a whole. Does the home reflect a sense of scale and proportion? Are some rooms too large, others too small? Does it have enough closet and storage space? Will the home heat and cool evenly? Or will it develop hot spots and cold spots? Is zone heating and cooling possible?

Now take stock. Bring all your thoughts together. Are the good looks merely show? Or are they integral to your needs and the design, function, and livability of the home?

Real estate agents love to show homes with "curb appeal." They like homes they can advertise as a "decorator's dream." Agents know most homebuyers prefer a home that looks good, a home they can show off to friends and relatives, a home they can be proud of. All of this is perfectly reasonable. Few buyers want a home that's considered the ugly duckling of the neighborhood. But when comparing houses, keep your reserve. Don't fall head over heels in love with appearance until after you've decided the home could live well for you and your family.

Mistake No. 69: *Our agent said it was a lot of house for the money.*

Lesson: *"A lot of house for the money" can sometimes mean "a lot of money for the house."*

"We had been looking for a two- or three-bedroom, two-bath house," recalls Tyrone Jones. "That size was all we needed or wanted. But our agent alerted us to a great bargain that had just come on the market. The house had four bedrooms, three baths, and a total of 2,400 square feet. At a price of $129,500, our agent told us it was really a lot of house for the money.

"Since I can't pass up a bargain," Tyrone continues, "we decided to take a look. Based on the price information our agent gave us, I figured we would buy this house for not much over $50 per square foot [p.s.f.]. Other houses we had considered were priced around $110,000 for 1,600 to 1,800 square feet. That works out roughly to $60 to $70 p.s.f. Compared to these other houses, the bigger one seemed cheap.

"And even though other houses were more in line with what we were hoping for, we didn't want to miss this deal. So we bought it. Looking back, I think that was the wrong decision. To buy the house, we pushed ourselves to the wall financially. Yet the house didn't give us the warmth and comfort we wanted. Besides, it costs too much time and money for upkeep. Instead of getting a lot of house for the money, we feel like we're paying a lot of money for the house."

Tyrone and his wife fell into the "bargain trap." They sacrificed their basic goals for a "good deal." When someone needs a good buy just to afford a house, shopping for a bargain makes sense. Or if you find a home that fills your most important needs and you buy it at a bargain price, that's even better. But think twice before you commit yourself. You don't want to simply grab a great deal. A home you enjoy is more important than any money you might "save."

Of course, whether an apparent "bargain-priced" home actually will save you money is a separate issue. To Tyrone, going for a price of $52 to $54 p.s.f. as compared to $60 to $70 p.s.f. seemed like a moneywise decision. But Tyrone later realized the larger home required higher property taxes, insurance, utilities, mortgage payments, and maintenance expenses. As his experience shows, you don't want to think just in terms of "a lot of house for the money." You need to figure the extra costs of owning the house over the years. Do you want to spend money for rarely used unnecessary space?

Just as important, be careful when you compare the per-square-foot costs of homes of different sizes, quality, and design.

- Smaller homes nearly always cost more per square foot than larger homes of the same quality. The expensive components of a house (baths, kitchen, heat and air, plumbing) generally don't increase proportionately as a home increases in size. In comparing large to small, the question should be whether the difference in price and operating costs makes the larger home a better buy than a smaller home.

- Dollars per square foot works best when you're comparing homes of the same size, amenities, and quality. Tyrone should have compared the p.s.f. price of the large home he bought to more similar homes. If he found other large homes typically sold for, say, $57 to $60 p.s.f., only then could he have reasonably concluded his home (at $52 p.s.f.) *may* present a bargain.

- Nonetheless, before coming to a final decision, Tyrone should have compared the homes according to their livability, energy efficiency, architectural style, and condition. Price per square foot is just one common denominator for comparing home prices. In valuing properties, appraisers certainly must make this type of calculation. But they also adjust the price per square foot up or down as warranted by a home's other important features.

Mistake No. 70:   *I didn't pay any attention to the fact that the home was sitting on two lots.*

Lesson: *An extra lot can mean extra value.*

Ralph Wozniak tells how he missed out on several hundred thousand dollars. "Some years back," says Ralph, "I was looking at houses in the older, well-established Point Grey neighborhood. My choice came down to two houses. One was sitting on a normal 33-foot lot. The other was built on a 50-foot site which included two 25-foot buildable lots. To my way of thinking, the houses were about equal in pros and cons. Both were priced at a little over $100,000. In the end, I bought the house with the 33-foot lot because I preferred its kitchen. The fact the other house was sitting on two buildable lots didn't affect my decision one way or the other. That was my mistake."

Here's what happened to make Ralph believe he should have factored the two lots into his decision. Four or five years after Ralph had bought, home prices in Point Grey started spiraling upward. They went from an entry level of around $90,000 up to around $200,000. Ralph recalls that at the time, he was feeling pretty happy with himself. His home had grown in value to around $225,000. Then he heard the two-lot house he had passed up just sold. The price was $395,000.

It wasn't the homes in Point Grey that were appreciating, it was the lots. This time around, the two-lot house was not sold to a homeowner. It was sold to a builder who promptly tore down the house on the site. In its place she built two houses—one on each lot. These two new homes sold for $475,000 each.

When Ralph considered his "home" to be worth around $225,000, he was wrong. His home was worth $25,000 to $35,000. His lot was worth $190,000 to $200,000. Remember: Homes seldom appreciate. Only in times of rapid inflation in construction costs will a house increase in (nominal) value. In most instances it's the land value that's going up. When you own two (buildable) lots, you double your chance for gain.

In hot markets homebuyers typically learn fast that a home with two lots means extra profit potential. They bid up its price. In slow markets, though, buyers frequently don't pay much attention. Since they don't expect appreciation, they're not willing to pay a premium for a two-lot house. To them, an extra-large site just means a bigger yard. This means that if you're buying in a slow (or uninformed) market, there's a good chance you can "buy" a second lot for a relatively small amount of money. Generally, the best places to look are older neighborhoods (especially those with strong potential for turnaround or otherwise moving upscale).

Depending on the way a home is situated on a two-lot site, you might even be able to put the extra lot to an immediate use. If the total size is big enough, you might subdivide the site. This would permit you to separate the extra lot from your home and sell it by itself. Or you might build another unit (house, cottage, carriage house) that you could rent out and hold as an investment. Given these additional opportunities, passing up a home with a second lot could be a mistake.

Mistake No. 71:   *We saw the house as a problem, not as an opportunity.*

Lesson: *Don't reject a home without fully considering whether you could make it work for you.*

To some homebuyers, shopping for a home seems like one frustration after another. If a house isn't too large, it's too small; or maybe it's too far of a commute to work, located in a less-desirable school district, needs too much work, lacks enough light, is too expensive, or has the wrong floor plan or architectural style. Whatever the home's features, these homebuyers can easily point out problems. They reject everything they look at because no home seems quite right.

I recall past friends of mine who went through this stage. Tom and Joan had been wanting to own their own home for more than two years. They earned good incomes and had enough for a down payment. They worked with good real estate agents. They diligently pored over the classified ads. And during two years of looking, they must have inspected 80 to 100 houses, maybe more. Yet they never bought.

Why? Because to them every home they inspected had some problem, defect, or flaw. Tom and Joan said they knew exactly what they wanted and wouldn't settle for anything less.

Although at the time my friends didn't realize it, the difficulty of their home search was not what they thought it was. They described their problem as "We just can't find what we're looking for." But their real difficulty was attitude. When they would walk into a house, they immediately began to find fault. In their mind's eye, they thought they could imagine exactly what they wanted; and if the house they were inspecting in some way violated their wish list, they rejected it—no ifs, ands, or buts.

Then one day when Tom was talking to me about the couple's inability to find a home, I abruptly changed the subject and asked, "Tom, why did you marry Joan? You've often complained that she's a little overweight, and she hates football. And you know she's always trying to get you to stop fishing and hunting."

As I finished, Tom immediately began to defend Joan, list her good points, and emphasize how well they got along together (which of course I knew). Then the light bulb flashed on in his mind. He stopped his praise of Joan and said, "All right, I see what you're getting at. I may not be perfect, and Joan may not be perfect, but we've still got a very good marriage. So why not stop insisting on the perfect house and find one that will work for us?"

"You got it," I answered.

Several months later Tom and Joan bought a triplex, renovated it, lived in it several years, sold it at a significant profit, and then built a custom-designed house. After they moved into their new house, I asked Tom, "Well, now that you've custom built your own house, do you have everything you wanted?"

Tom smiled and said, "Has Joan lost weight? No. Have I stopped watching six football games a week? No. Do we have the perfect house? No. We love each other and we love the house, but nothing's perfect."

Getting frustrated shopping and comparing homes? Then think of Tom and Joan. Shift your sights from what's wrong with a house to what's right—or could be made right. Much of this chapter does describe mistakes in home buying that commonly result from failing to spot a home's defects, flaws, or features that don't suit your needs. But you can also err by becoming too critical and rejecting houses too quickly. Try to strike a happy balance. Don't just list problems. Look for ways you might be able to make a less than perfect home work for you. You can always trade up later.

Chapter 6

Negotiate Your Purchase Agreement

Mistake No. 72:   *We thought our agent represented us.*

Lesson: *Before you begin to work with an agent, set ground rules for your relationship.*

For the past several years "who represents whom" has ranked as one of the most controversial issues in home buying. Until the early 1990s nearly all real estate agents were employed by sellers to find buyers for their homes. Under this traditional system you may have worked with an agent who advised, counseled, and helped you negotiate your home purchase. But as a matter of law and contract, that agent was most likely a subagent of the sellers—not "your" agent. Here's how the traditional system worked and why it's now sparking so much controversy and confusion.

Under the traditional system, a seller might sign a listing contract with Fox Realty. In turn, Fox Realty would forward this listing to a multiple listing service (MLS). The MLS probably included dozens of other real estate agencies who in total employed hundreds, maybe thousands, of real estate agents. To carry through this example, let's say one of these other cooperating realty firms is Hoosier Realty, and Joe Salesman works for Hoosier Realty as a sales agent. You've met Joe through your local chamber of commerce meetings, or maybe a friend of yours recommended him.

You call Joe. He then sets up a meeting where you discuss some preliminaries, such as your housing needs, your finances, how much you're willing to invest in a home, and the locations you think you prefer. With this information, Joe's likely to suggest some homes to show you. If all goes well, you find a home you like and you tell Joe you want to make an offer. Joe advises you about the price, terms, conditions, and contingencies to be included and then helps you negotiate a purchase agreement with the sellers through their listing agent, Sally Saleswoman, who's employed by Fox Realty. After some give and take, you and the sellers find common ground and strike a deal. Everyone's satisfied.

Now what's wrong with the way this transaction was handled? Your agent, Joe, was representing you and looking out for your interests. Sally was representing the sellers and advising them about their interests. Or at least that's the way it may seem.

But, in fact, under the traditional system of brokerage, Joe didn't represent you. As a salesman with Hoosier Realty, a firm that had joined with Fox Realty as a cooperating broker, Joe was legally a subagent of the sellers. According to the sellers' listing agreement, the MLS cooperating brokerage contract, and the law of the agency, Joe owed his allegiance to the sellers—not to you.

As a matter of law, Joe was required to relay to the sellers your statements like "We just have to have the house. It's the best one we've looked at by far." Or; "Let's try an offer of $87,500, but we'll go to $95,000 if we have to." Or perhaps the sellers learned you had told Joe, "We're really pressed for time. Our apartment lease is ending and this is the only house we've looked at where the sellers are willing to give an early possession date." Or maybe from the opposite direction, you believed Joe was sincere when he told you "the sellers won't budge. Their absolute low dollar is $95,000." So thinking you had no choice, you paid $95,000.

Now, how would you feel if you later learned the sellers were really experiencing a cash crunch and were so eager to sell they would have accepted a price of $85,000 for their home? Yet your agent, Joe, the man you trusted enough to share your confidences, never mentioned this fact to you. In effect, Joe's silence kept you from learning this choice bit of information that would have greatly increased your negotiating power. How would you feel? You would probably feel angry and cheated. After all, Joe led you to believe he was representing you, but in reality he was working as an agent of the "enemy." You might even think about suing Joe for fraud and deception.

And that's exactly what Sheila and Jeff Buck have done. The Bucks

have sued their agent for fraud because "We thought our agent represented us, when she really was working for the sellers. Had Diane told
us she was duty bound to the sellers, we never would have told her
our top dollar. We're sure she used the information against us."

To help you and other homebuyers prevent the mistake of the Bucks
(and their agent), nearly all states have recently enacted some type of
agency disclosure laws. In addition to agency disclosure, state laws
and the National Association of Realtors are making it easier for you
to use a "buyer's broker" or "buyer's agent" when you shop for a
home or negotiate a purchase agreement.

Under these new laws, licensed real estate agents are supposed to
disclose to you the types of agency relationships that are legal in your
state, explain their meaning, and then give you a choice. Although
state laws differ, in general, you might have three or four choices.

1. You can elect the traditional system where you work with an agent
    or subagent of the sellers.

2. You can choose dual agency. Here the agent helps both sellers and
    buyers, but agrees not to divulge confidential information that
    could give one party an unfair advantage over the other.

3. You may employ a facilitator. A facilitator owes no fiduciary re-
    sponsibility to either you or the sellers. He or she would act more
    as a mediator. The idea is to find agreement, not to represent either
    buyer or sellers.

4. As a fourth and growing option, you might use a buyer's agent
    who should represent your interest exclusively. Buyer's agents
    can't legally release your confidential information to the sellers.
    But they can pass along to you any information about the sellers
    they know that could strengthen your hand in negotiations.

Although I can't go into all the pros and cons of each of these types
of agency relationships (that would require another book), my primary purpose here is to alert you to the fact "your" agent may be
working for the sellers. Also, many state laws don't require agents to
disclose until you're ready to make an offer on a property. By that time
you may have already revealed your finances, how well you like the
house, or that your landlord has ended your lease and you have to find
someplace else to live within the next 60 days.

So, here's the best advice to follow: Set ground rules for your relationship *before* you begin to work with a real estate agent. Each type of
agency has its own advantages and disadvantages. As long as you

know the ground rules for what you can disclose and what you should keep to yourself, you can work with any type of agent. Mistakes are most likely to occur when you simply assume "your" agent is really your agent.

In addition, take into account an agent's character, competence, and knowledge. The specific agent you choose to work with stands just as important as the type of your agency relationship. In my experience, I've found most real estate professionals—men and women who are committed to a career in real estate—don't view home buying and home selling as an adversarial contest.

Buying (or selling) a home is not like filing a lawsuit. In contrast to lawyers whose so-called "ethics" permit them to mislead and deceive, consumer laws (as well as professional Realtor ethics and personal reputation) oblige real estate agents to treat all buyers and sellers fairly and honestly. Although buyer's agency may be the wave of the future, historically the great majority of homebuyers have been served well by the traditional agency system. The key, then, to buying a home succcessfully is to locate a true real estate professional and then to fully discuss the type of agency that will govern your relationship.

Mistake No. 73:   *I tried to buy directly from an owner to save the commission but instead lost $5,000.*

Lesson: *Buying without an agent can cost you more than you save. Be careful.*

When Danny Boatman decided to stop renting and buy his own home, he contacted several real estate agents whose names he had seen on for-sale signs. "They didn't impress me much," says Danny. "One just wanted to talk all the time, but never listened. Another one kept showing me houses and neighborhoods he didn't know anything about. I'd ask him questions and he would answer, 'I dunno, but I can find out for you if you want.' This was a hassle I didn't need.

"So I decided to concentrate on for sale by owners. That way I wouldn't have to deal with agents, and I could get the sellers to give me a lower price since they would be saving the commission. It seemed like a smart move. Unfortunately, I got suckered. My smart move cost me $5,000. That's a mistake I won't make again."

Danny actually made not one but several mistakes. First, for all practical purposes, he selected his agents randomly. He might as well as flipped open the yellow pages to the real estate section, pressed his finger to the page, and started telephoning. The chances are that if Danny or anyone else merely pulls an agent's name out of the telephone book or off a for-sale sign, they're not going to come with a first-class professional. Real estate sales follows the same 80-20 rule found in most fields. The bottom 80 percent of the agents do 20 percent of the business, and the top 20 percent of the agents do 80 percent of the business.

To locate a real estate professional, ask relatives or friends for recommendations. Read the newspapers for names of top producers. Call the sales manager of the most highly regarded real estate firms and find out who among their agents has provided the highest quality services to the most buyers. In other words, work with an agent who has a proven track record. Helping people buy and sell homes requires a great deal of knowledge, competence, and, quite often, creativity. You don't want a chauffeur. You need a pro. Danny Boatman failed to understand this critical difference.

Second, Danny mistakenly assumed that if he bought direct from an owner he would get a better price. Since the owners wouldn't have to pay a commission, they could pass along their savings to him. But why would they want to? Most sellers don't take on the burden and expense of selling their own home so they can give buyers a better price. They do it to pocket more money for themselves.

In fact, as often as not, people selling their own homes overprice them. They're hoping to find some "bargain-hunting" buyers who will be hoodwinked into believing they are saving money because there's no agent involved. In addition, even if the home appears to be priced right, it may suffer from hidden defects. In today's lawsuit-happy world, professional agents will insist that sellers disclose their home's shortcomings. Owners who sell on their own, in contrast, are noted for "forgetting" about the erratic furnace or the fuses that blow every time the toaster and microwave are turned on at the same time.

Third, here's how Danny lost his $5,000. After negotiating the basic price and terms of their purchase agreement, the sellers asked Danny for an earnest money deposit of $5,000. This amount would be credited against his down payment at closing after Danny had arranged his mortgage financing. Danny knew earnest money deposits were customary, and since he planned to put a total of $15,000 down, a $5,000 good faith deposit didn't seem unreasonable. So he wrote the sellers a check. That was his biggest mistake.

As it turned out, Danny could not get his financing approved within the 30 days allowed by his purchase agreement. To make matters even more difficult for Danny, other buyers wanted the house and they were already preapproved by their lender. The sellers gave Danny an extra week to close, but to no avail. He couldn't close. The sellers went ahead and sold to the other buyers.

When Danny asked for his deposit back, the sellers told him they would send him a check after the other buyers completed their purchase. Should that new deal fall through for some unexpected reason, they promised to give Danny another chance to come up with his financing. Danny reluctantly agreed because he really wanted the house. But the new sale did close. The sellers moved to Tacoma. And Danny never saw his $5,000 check.

Danny then hired an attorney who wrote the sellers and demanded them to return his deposit. The sellers' attorney responded by saying that Danny had forfeited the deposit when they had given him extra time and yet he still couldn't get his financing put together.

Danny disagreed. "We didn't discuss anything about forfeiture," Danny told his attorney. "Well," the attorney said, "we can sue them in federal court. But that will cost you a lot more than $5,000, and I can't guarantee you'll win, or that if you win, you can actually collect. There's not really anything I can do. You might as well kiss your $5,000 good-bye."

No one would deny that, on occasion, you can negotiate directly with sellers and save yourself some money. (Or maybe the home you like best isn't listed with an agent.) But if that's the route you choose, be careful. Remember this advice:

1. If you buy direct, you'll be giving up not only the services agents provide to help you find a home, but also the very important services that carry you through from purchase contract to obtaining financing to closing.

2. Get the home professionally inspected for condition and appraised for value. Take especial care if the sellers are offering you easy financing.

3. Employ an attorney highly experienced in home-buying transactions to help you negotiate and draw up a purchase agreement. In addition to checking the contract terms, no attorney would ever let you give money directly to the sellers. Rather, your deposit money should go into an escrow account for safekeeping.

Mistake No. 74: *We didn't know we could withdraw our offer.*

Lesson: You may withdraw your offer at any time before the sellers accept it.

As you prepare your offer to purchase a home, you'll have to decide how long you want to give the sellers to accept it. Commonly used real estate sales contracts include a clause that reads something like:

> This offer prepared and delivered to the Sellers by the Buyers on _____, 19_____, at _____ and shall remain open for _____ days, or until revoked by the Buyers.

In regard to this clause, some homebuyers overlook or misunderstand the meaning of the last six words. In effect, these words give you the right to withdraw your offer any time before the sellers have accepted it. If you tell the sellers you'll leave your offer open for three days, but then change your mind for any reason whatsoever, simply notify your agent (preferably in writing, but that's not essential). Even if your contract doesn't include these words or something similar, you still may withdraw your offer.

On occasion, agents forget to fully explain your right to withdraw. Some agents don't like to emphasize the point because homebuyers (especially first-time buyers) often get second thoughts about the wisdom of their decision to buy. To squelch these worries, the agent might gloss over your right to pull back. He or she might lead you to believe you're obliged to keep the offer on the table for the specified number of days.

Of course, you shouldn't withdraw just because you start focusing on what might go wrong. Such thoughts are natural. You should get rid of negative emotions by replacing them with thoughts of how much you're going to enjoy the home and home ownership. But if you discover new information (you're getting transferred or you've noticed a shortfall in your bank balance), or you run across another home that better fits your needs, then you might want to exercise your right of withdrawal.

Also, keep in mind that if the sellers change any part of your offer, you're released from obligation. Any counteroffer kills a previous offer. Should you offer $69,500 and the seller counters with a price of $69,501, your bid of $69,500 is dead. You could bring it back to life if you wanted. But if you reject the sellers' $69,501, they can't unilaterally declare (without your agreement), "Okay, then, we'll accept $69,500."

From a negotiating standpoint, you generally want to keep the sellers guessing about what you plan to do. Let them know you're considering other options. The sellers should realize that if they wait too long to accept your offer or if they counter too high, they could lose you as a prospective buyer.

Mistake No. 75: *We never even met the sellers. We didn't know anything about them.*

Lesson: *Get to know as much as you can about the sellers.*

Some real estate agents do everything they can to keep buyers and sellers away from each other. For good reason. Agents have seen too many potential deals fall through because of personality clashes. Or they fear that sellers (since agents in the past have nearly always represented sellers) might give away a choice bit of information that will help the other party.

"Why are you selling?" the buyers ask.

"Oh, Mack's been transferred," the sellers respond, "we have to be in Omaha by the end of next month."

Although the keep-the-buyers-and-sellers-apart sales strategy sometimes is best for sellers, as a rule I don't recommend it for buyers. Before you make your first offer, you want to learn all you can about the sellers. What kind of people are they? Do they seem generous and open? Or are they rigid and argumentative? Do they take a great deal of pride in their home? Are they moving reluctantly; or are they eager to leave? Have they already bought another home? Why are they selling? What are their most important needs: emotional, personal, financial? What are their worries and concerns?

The sellers aren't really trying to sell a house. They're actually reaching for more distant goals. Selling their home is a means to those ends. Naturally, then, the sellers won't judge the price and terms of your offer by absolute standards. They will judge it according to how well it helps them move toward what they are ultimately trying to achieve. That's why it's a big mistake not to get to know the sellers. Without understanding their real needs, you may miss a great opportunity to find high value/low value trade-offs that can benefit both of you.

Let's say the sellers had previously accepted two offers that both fell through because the buyers couldn't come up with financing. With these experiences providing background context, the sellers may be quite anxious. They don't want to be strung out again. So if you can assure them you have the money to buy (bank statements, credit report, lender preapproval letter, job security), they most likely would be willing to give you a lower price.

In fact, all too frequently, homebuyers and sellers aim most of their negotiating power toward price. The sellers want a higher price. The buyers want a lower price. Stalemate. Don't get caught in this trap. To prevent it—or escape from it—you need to meet the sellers, talk with them, and learn all you can about their perceptions, past home-selling experiences, feelings, and needs. But agent concerns about personality clashes are valid. So when meeting and talking with the sellers, don't stray too far from these guidelines:

- Meet the sellers as soon as possible. The sooner you get a fix on who they are and what they're like, the better you can begin to map your negotiation strategy. Also, sellers are generally more open with information when you first look at a home. At that point they're eager to please. They want to excite your interest. If you wait to meet them until after you've made an offer, they'll be guarding their disclosures more closely.

- Get as many concessions as you can before you ever begin negotiations. "You're asking $125,000, is that right? Just so we can fairly compare the price of your home to others were looking at, have you thought about how much less you would accept?" Or: "You're asking $125,000, right? Can you tell me what personal property (appliances, drapes, rugs, patio furniture, gazebo, etc.) you're willing to include?" Or maybe: "Have you considered how much you're willing to carry back in a note?" By "innocently" suggesting concessions in this way, you're not "negotiating" with the sellers. You're not really even asking for concessions. You're merely trying to gather information so you can fairly rank the sellers' home against other houses that are up for sale. Sensing you are exploring other options, many sellers will sweeten the deal before you write your first offer.

- Inquire, don't interrogate. The way you ask your questions is far more important than the questions themselves. Phrase them as innocuously as you can. Don't intimidate, accuse, threaten, or debate. Remember Peter Falk as Columbo, the perpetually "disoriented" detective. Columbo didn't interrogate suspects. He gently probed. Use similar tactics. Encourage the easy flow of information. Don't try to extract it.

- Don't talk exclusively about the house or the sellers. Establish rapport. Try to find other common ground. Talk about the last Cubs game or that old favorite, the weather (certainly not politics, perhaps religion or ethnicity, if you share a common faith or cultural heritage). Negotiations are about people, not money. Treat the sellers as people, not merely owners of a house you might want to buy.

- Compliment, don't criticize. As you walk through the sellers' home, sincerely compliment their beautiful grandfather clock. "Does it have an interesting history? How long have you owned it?" Comment on other belongings they seem to take pride in. Have the owners decorated or remodeled their home with taste, flair, or creativity? If so, tell them. What about the yard? Do the sellers have a green thumb? Can you genuinely admire their tomatoes or roses?

   At this first meeting, prevent picking out flaws. Develop a cordial attitude. Establish a *relationship* bank account so you will have something to draw on later if (when) you need it. To sharply criticize the sellers' home won't loosen them up to accept a lower price. But it may very well turn them against you and make later negotiations more difficult. (Of course, also corral those enthusiastic exclamations: "Wow! This is exactly what we want. It's so much nicer than the other houses we've seen.")

- Share information about yourself with the sellers. Let them get to know you. Skip the bravado. But accent personal characteristics that tell the sellers you're decent, credible people who like (not love) their home. Creating trust and building a relationship can't travel a one-way street.

Mistake No. 76:   *The worst they can do is say no.*

Lesson: *The worst they can do is say get lost.*

Nothing destroys trust faster than a lowball offer. When you lowball the sellers, you signal you're going for a win-lose negotiating strategy with the sellers as the losers.

Joan McGill recalls her lowball experience. "We really wanted this house," says Joan. "But my husband considered himself a hot-shot negotiator. So even though the house was priced just a little over market at $129,000, he convinced me we should start with an offer of $95,000. 'All they can say is no,' he assured me. 'At the worst, they'll probably compromise. We can still get the house at a bargain price of around $110,000 to $112,000.' Well, he clearly missed that one. We got the house all right—at a price of $129,000." After our lowball offer, the sellers simply refused to negotiate with us. They just said, 'The price is $129,000. Take it or leave it.' So we ate crow and took it."

Most sellers are emotionally involved with their homes. A lowball offer insults them. Besides, if the sellers are listed with a real estate agent, they've got a good idea of what their home is worth. And if they doubt the agent's price, nine times out of 10 the sellers figure higher, not lower. So what chance does a lowball offer have of getting accepted? Slim and none.

Put yourself in the sellers' shoes. Your home is worth $120,000 to $125,000. Out of the blue, someone offers you $95,000. How would you respond? You'd probably think: (1) the buyers don't know what they're doing, so why even talk with them; (2) they think we're so ignorant we don't know the value of our own home, and they're trying to take advantage of us; (3) the buyers believe we're desperate and they want to prey on our misfortune; or (4) the buyers aren't serious buyers. They are just shotgunning lowball offers to see what might turn up. (In fact, this tactic is taught in some of the get-rich-in-real-estate seminars.)

Anyway you look at it, buyers who lowball destroy trust. They destroy the possibility of working out a win-win purchase agreement. Most sellers respond to a lowball by flat out rejecting it, counteroffering at the full asking price, or telling the buyers to get lost. "Stop wasting our time!" This is not to say you'll never find ignorant or desperate sellers who will accept a lowball offer. But as Joan McGill and her husband learned, as a negotiating ploy for a home you would like to own, lowballing is generally a mistake.

Mistake No. 77:   *We thought the sellers had accepted our offer.*

Lesson: *Get the sellers' signatures on the contract.*

"We had been going back and forth with offers and counteroffers," says Keith Zine. "We kept trying to find that magic combination of price and terms that would click for both of us. Finally it seemed like we found it. We were working with our agent in her office late Friday afternoon and she came up with a solution that would work for us. Next she called the sellers' agent to ask him to run it by the sellers before we wrote it up in a revised contract. About 20 minutes later the sellers' agent called back. He said we had a deal. The sellers could live with our solution.

"Our agent printed out a new copy of the agreement. We signed it, and she said she would drop by the sellers later that evening to get their signatures. 'Congratulations,' she told us. 'You've just bought a great house. I know you're going to be happy with it.' We were elated.

"But our spirits came crashing down less than 24 hours later. That's when we learned the sellers had accepted another much better offer that an agent from another firm brought them on Saturday morning. Our agent had dropped the ball. She hadn't kept her 7:00 P.M. appointment with the sellers. Because of a personal conflict, she had rescheduled the appointment for 1:00 o'clock Saturday afternoon. By that time the sellers had already accepted the other offer with the provision we would be given a chance to match it. We couldn't. So we lost the house."

The lesson here is very simple. In real estate, never assume you have a deal until you have a signed contract. An oral acceptance isn't binding. Once upon a time you could count on people to honor their word—regardless of whether it had been committed to writing. But to a great extent, those days are gone. To be safe, if you receive an oral commitment to an agreement you want to see fulfilled, get the necessary signatures as fast as possible. Don't give the sellers time to change their minds, change the terms, or find a better offer.

Mistake No. 78:   *The listing handout said "wet bar/sink" included.*

Lesson: *Itemize in writing all personal property and fixtures included in the sale.*

Exactly what are you buying when you buy a home? Does the sales price include that $1,500 Tiffany light fixture hanging over the dining room table? Does it include the gazebo in the backyard? Does it include drapes, rugs, carpeting, appliances, or the window air conditioner? Does it include the mailbox? What about the light bulbs in the ceiling lights and outdoor flood lamps?

"We couldn't believe it," recalls Jay Martin. "We got into town after dark around 8:00 o'clock. We went right to our newly-bought house eager to spend our first night there even though the moving van wasn't scheduled to arrive until the next day. We opened the front door, reached for the light switch, and flipped it on. Nothing happened. At first we thought the electric company had turned off the power. But when we felt our way to the kitchen, we could hear the refrigerator running. We opened the door to the fridge expecting to get some light, nothing happened. Like lost souls in the dark, we wandered from room to room, flipping on every light switch we could find. Still no light. Finally we borrowed a flashlight from a neighbor, and we quickly discovered the problem. The sellers had taken every light bulb in the house with them—including the bulbs from inside the refrigerator."

When Forrest and Dyan Albertson bought their home, the Realtor handout that described the features of the house listed a "wet bar/ sink." In looking at the home before they bought, the Albertsons recalled admiring the bar, its fine quality wood, and its unique design. In fact, they had complimented the owners on the bar.

But when the Albertsons moved into their new home, the bar was gone. The only evidence remaining were the imprints on the floor showing where the bar had stood. "Where's the bar?" Forrest demanded of his real estate agent.

"Oh," she said, "that was the sellers' personal property. The bar wasn't included in the sale."

"What do you mean, 'not included'?" Forrest shot back. "The handout you gave us listing the features of the house said wet bar/sink!"

"That doesn't refer to the bar," the agent said. "That referred to the wet bar sink. You get the sink, not the bar. That bar was worth over $1,000."

I once bought a house that had a large antique mirror bolted to the bricks above the mantel on the fireplace. When I took possession of the house, the mirror and the bolts were gone. I got the holes where the bolts had been.

Each of these stories teaches the same lesson: Never assume the sellers plan to leave any specific property with the house. Sellers have been known to remove items as trivial as light bulbs and mailboxes. At times, they remove items of high value, such as chandeliers, gazebos, and wet bars. They may even take things that are bolted to the floors, walls, or ceilings. There have even been court cases where after contracting with buyers, sellers have removed toilets and furnaces. No matter how obvious it is that the item belongs with the house, the sellers may in fact entertain different ideas.

In some instances the sellers simply show their pettiness. In others the sellers interpret ambiguity in their own favor. And sometimes sellers take things they know rightfully belong to the buyers. But they may justify their actions with "those buyers stole the house from us, so it's only right we even the score." Or with larceny in their hearts and a keen sense of the impractical, the sellers may say to themselves, "What are the buyers gonna do, come to North Dakota to get us?"

There is a body of law (real property, fixtures, personal property) that attempts to define "what stays" and "what goes" in a home-buying transaction. Like all law, though, it's riddled with contradictions, conflicting court opinions, and gray areas—not to mention the difficult and expensive burdens of using lawyers to enforce a claim, even when you're sure the law favors your view. (I believe there's a Yiddish curse that says, "May you have a lawsuit you believe you can win." You might also recall Dickens's *Bleak House*.)

The law may offer recourse but rarely satisfaction. The best way to prevent mistakes of "what goes" and "what stays" is to assume nothing. Write out a complete list of everything you intend to be included in the home's sales price. Go through the house room by room with the sellers and your real estate agent. Identify, itemize, and list. Your goal is to leave no chance for doubt, confusion, or ambiguity. Then attach the signed list to both your copy and the sellers' copy of the purchase agreement.

Never depend on an oral promise of the sellers. "You're such a nice couple," the sellers say, "and since we no longer have any use for them in our new house, we'll leave you the washer and dryer. They're old, but they'll serve you until you can buy your own."

Of course, when making their promise to you, the sellers may not know their daughter also needs a washer and dryer. But where will these appliances end up when the daughter says, "Mom, you know I hate going to the laundromat. If you're giving your washer and dryer away, you should give them to me." At that point, if you haven't written the washer and dryer into your purchase agreement, even the most well-intentioned sellers may be tempted to help their daughter at your expense.

Mistake No. 79: *We fell in love with the house and just had to have it.*

Lesson: Keep your love to yourself. Put your options on the table.

In his best-selling book *You Can Get Anything You Want,* Roger Dawson, the world-renowned negotiating expert, tells how a negotiation slipup cost him $30,000 when he was buying his family's present home. Roger writes that one day while teaching his daughter to drive in the secluded hills of Southern California, he spied the house of his dreams. "Everything about the house was perfect," he says, "and it was for sale."

Posing as a reluctant, if not altogether indifferent, buyer, Roger relates how he plotted his negotiation strategy—only to see it evaporate when his wife and daughter returned to look at the house without him. "They oohed and aahed over every feature, and by the time they were through with their tour, they had demolished my reluctant buyer plan," says Roger.

It also didn't help matters when his wife told the sellers Roger really thought their house was wonderful. At that point the sellers knew the Dawsons were hooked. With a ticket price of $15, Roger says many people think a tour of Hearst Castle at San Simeon is expensive. But he calculated that one house tour by his wife and daughter cost him $30,000.

When talking with sellers, you've got to walk a fine line. Yes, you want to show interest, develop a cooperative, problem-solving attitude, and prevent critical remarks that may offend. Yet you can't go overboard with lavish praise. Nor do you want to tell yourself "This is the perfect house, we've simply got to have it."

In other words, don't shut out other options—either in your own mind or in the eyes of the sellers. When the sellers believe you've eliminated other houses from consideration, they'll naturally use that information to bolster their own position. Should you tell yourself "Nothing else will do," you abandon the strongest negotiating power any buyer has—the willpower to walk away from the deal. Sometimes emotions do get the better of us. But keep in mind that once you relinquish your "walk away willpower," you might as well hand the sellers a blank contract and let them fill in the numbers.

Mistake No. 80:   *Our negotiations centered too much on price.*

Lesson: *To most sellers, price is the main event. It's up to you to win agreement by emphasizing other important points.*

"The mistake many home sellers make," says Realtor Bill Sloane, "is that they stop listening if the purchase price offer is too low." Realtor Sloane is pointing out a well-known fact. To most sellers, price is the main event. Everything else is intermission. That's why lowball offers can so easily knock negotiations off the track before they even get revved up.

However, if you realize this fact, you can often use it to your advantage. By not pushing the sellers too hard on price, you sometimes can get nearly anything else you want. Let me illustrate with one of my own home-buying experiences from some years ago.

In this instance, the sellers and I were sitting at their dining room table going through a form contract point by point. The first point was price. Although the sellers had their house priced fairly, I offered $5,000 less. The sellers rejected. I said, "Well, let's put that issue on hold, and see if we can agree on some of the other points." In abbreviated form, here's how those other points went.

- The sellers agreed to a lease-purchase plan with closing 15 months after I took possession of the property.
- The sellers agreed to a cash deposit of just $2,500.
- They agreed to give possession within six weeks.

- They agreed to let me store all my household furniture in their den (Florida room) for the month prior to my taking possession of the property. (I had sold my previous home and was giving quick possession to the buyers, so I was going "homeless" for a month.)
- The sellers agreed to include in the sale about $2,000 worth of furniture and appliances.

These people were the easiest sellers I had ever dealt with. But when we eventually returned to price, they still didn't want to budge. Then finally after we talked some more, the husband said, "Look, here's what we paid for the property. At what you're offering us, we would take a $3,000 loss. We want to at least get what we paid."

Now, here's where negotiation experts differ. Some would say at this point you've got the sellers committed to everything but price. Hang tough and you can still get the price concession you want. The sellers are so close to a deal, they won't let you walk away. If they did, they would just have to start over again with someone else—if and when that someone else appears. If they're smart, the sellers won't take that risk.

For reasons explained later (see Mistake No. 83), I don't endorse this view. If the sellers have been willing to yield on every point that's important to me, why not let them score a point too? Besides, once you've gotten nearly all you want, why push so hard you might upset the entire applecart? So following a win-win approach, I increased my offer by $3,500 on the promise the sellers would take responsibility for cutting down and removing a dead tree from the backyard. They quickly agreed. We had a deal we were both happy with.

Now, let's go back to the beginning of the negotiations. What would have happened early on if we had heavily debated price? Even if I had been able to pull the sellers down to my offer, that "success" probably would have destroyed my chances of getting all the other things I needed to make the deal work. A hollow victory indeed.

On other occasions, though, I have reversed this approach somewhat. When through my early inquiries I've learned the sellers have needs stronger than price, I emphasize how I am willing to help them meet those needs (e.g., their preferred possession date, their need to know the transaction's actually going to close). Then once the sellers understand they are receiving nearly all the terms and conditions they want, I feel I can justify my request for their concession on price.

The important thing for you to remember is that sellers don't demand their price for purely economic reasons. For many, price is laden with emotional content. A low offer doesn't just hurt their pocketbook. It affronts their psyche.

Should you enter negotiations with the idea you're negotiating price alone, more than likely one party will "lose" and the other party will "win." On the other hand, when you adopt the view you are negotiating (searching for) an *agreement*, you and sellers can both emerge winners.

Mistake No. 81:   *"Split the difference" sounds like a good compromise to me.*

Lesson: *Don't compromise, conciliate.*

In negotiation lore, the story is frequently told of a mother who hears her two children bickering at the dinner table. Each child wants the one remaining slice of cake. Tiring of this debate, the mother takes the cake, slices it in two, and gives half to Craig and half to Shawn. "There," she says, "as you get older you must realize you can't have everything you want. You must learn to compromise. Remember this as an important lesson."

This well-intentioned mother thought she was teaching her kids a valuable lesson, whereas, in fact, she had imprinted them with one of the greatest obstacles to win-win negotiating. By "splitting the difference" before fully exploring her children's wants and a wide range of options, this mother mistakenly framed her kids' debate along a single continuum. Compromise simply meant deciding how much cake to give each child.

On the other hand, had the mother framed the problem multidimensionally, more than likely she could have formulated a better solution. What if one child really preferred the icing? What if the children shared a television set and each preferred different programs? What if the children shared after dinner-cleanup responsibilities? What if the children had money from an allowance? What if Shawn didn't really want the cake, but simply liked to annoy Craig?

Had the mother recognized a wider range of potential wants, trade-offs, and outcomes, she may have produced results more satisfying (or just) for both children. The true art of negotiating doesn't depend on one's readiness to strike a compromise. Instead it depends on seeing beyond a single issue stretching across a one-dimensional, either-or continuum.

Earlier (see Mistake No. 80) I told how the sellers I was buying a home from agreed to let me use one of the rooms in their home to store my household furniture instead of an earlier date of possession which would have better met my needs. But what if we had simply focused our negotiations on possession date? I would have said, "I have to be out of my present home on February 1st. So I need possession on that date."

The sellers may have responded, "But we can't get into our new home until March 1. A February 1 possession date is out of the question. We can't possibly give you possession before February 28.

"Okay," I might say if I'm thinking compromise, "let's split the difference. I'll agree to February 15. I'm willing to meet you halfway."

Although meeting the sellers halfway has the ring of justice, reason, and fair play, in many situations, either it simply doesn't make sense, or it overlooks another more satisfying outcome. In this case, February 15 was actually undesirable for both of us. So that "position" never even found its way onto the table. By looking at my real problem— What am I going to do with my furniture for a month without incurring the high costs of multiple moves into and out of storage?—we struck upon the solution of storing my household goods in a large room they used, but didn't really need. We both were satisfied with this outcome.

Nine times out of 10, conciliation beats compromise. And this was one of them.

I might add here another point that works against compromise as a desirable negotiating strategy. People who go into negotiations with a compromise mind-set too often want to begin their negotiations at the extreme. Naturally, if you believe the sellers will split the difference, it's to your advantage to offer $95,000 for a $120,000 house. Should the sellers accept your meet-you-halfway tactic, they will sell you the house for $107,500.

But few sellers are that obliging. The tactic of bid low and compromise is too familiar and obvious to work effectively. As negotiating expert Herb Cohen likes to emphasize, "A tactic perceived is no tactic at all." You're far more likely to negotiate successfully if you bake a bigger cake. Expand your knowledge of wants, needs, trade-offs, and possibilities. To paraphrase Emerson, "Foolish compromises are the hobgoblins of little minds."

Mistake No. 82: *We let our agent negotiate for us.*

Lesson: Use an agent as an intermediary but negotiate for yourself.

Writing in *Real Estate Today*, a national trade magazine for Realtors, sales agent Sal Gebbia tells of an offer he received on one of his listings. Sal says that after receiving the purchase offer from a *buyer's agent*, this agent told Sal, "This is their [first] offer, but I know my buyers will go up to $150,000."

"Of course," Sal adds, "I told my sellers that information and we were pleased with the outcome of the transaction."

The lesson here is very plain. Never let your agent do your negotiating for you. Don't give your agent information you do not want the other side to learn. Don't let on to your agent that you're willing to pay a higher price than your first offer. Use your agent as a fact finder and intermediary. But guard your emotions, confidences, and intentions.

Many buyers (especially first-timer buyers) mistakenly rely too heavily on their agents to actually come up with the terms of their offer and carry out their negotiations. These buyers will ask their agents, "What price do you think I should offer? What's the most you think I should pay? Will the sellers pay points or agree to carry-back financing?" Then the buyers follow whatever the agent recommends. Unfortunately, these buyers who shy away from their negotiating responsibilities and rely too heavily on their agents run the following risks.

YOU MAY BE WORKING WITH A SUBAGENT

In many instances, remember, you will be working with the sellers' subagent. As a subagent, "your" Realtor's legal duty is to the seller. Thus, in favoring the sellers' interests, the agent may persuade you to enhance the price or terms of your offer. Or the agent may disclose your confidences to the sellers.

Now, as a practical matter, many "subagents" don't strictly follow the letter of the law. Even though technically they're representing sellers, in their heart and efforts they may feel more loyalty to you. I know many "subagents" who work harder on behalf of buyers than they do sellers.

Nevertheless, since you can't be sure how the agent will use the information you share, guard your disclosures carefully. Also, when it comes to your offering price and terms, rely on your agent for facts about the sellers, neighborhood statistics, selling prices of comp houses, and general market conditions. Listen to the agent's price recommendations and accept the benefits of his or her experience. But don't delegate your decision making. You may be led into paying more than you need to.

BE CAUTIOUS OF BUYERS' AGENTS

In trying to recruit business, a number of brokerage firms and sales agents have been promoting "buyers' agency." According to this view, since sellers are represented by their own agents, buyers also need someone to look out for their interests. Marilyn Williams, a Vancouver, Washington, real estate broker, says, "Buyers should think of their agents as attorneys. Would you want to have one attorney representing both parties in a divorce settlement?"

Superficially, the idea sounds reasonable, and there's little doubt the number of buyers' agents is going to grow very fast through the remainder of the 1990s. Even if you choose to employ a buyers' agent, however, you still need to guard your disclosures and negotiating strategy carefully. First of all, like the agent Sal Gebbia referred to earlier, even buyers' agents may disclose your confidences—either intentionally or unintentionally.

Second, we're all subject to subtle influences. A buyers' agent may talk you into offering a higher price or better terms because it will make his or her job easier. For example, in which case do you think your agent will work hardest for you: When the agent knows you've offered $85,000, but you've said you're willing to go up to $92,500? Or when you offer $85,000 and say "If they don't accept this offer, I'd like to go out and look at four or five other houses."

WATCH WHAT YOU SAY

Regardless of whether you're working with a sellers' subagent, a buyers' agent, a dual agent, or a facilitator, you should watch what you say. Don't tell your agent everything and then turn the negotiations over to her with the simple instructions, "Do the best job you can," or "Why don't you try $135,000 and if that doesn't fly, we can go to $140,000?"

In fact, it doesn't matter whether we're talking about lawyers, insurance agents, financial planners, Real estate sales persons, or any other type of agency relationship, conflict of interest always lurks in the background. As a general rule, you've got to walk a fine line. Release enough information to achieve the results you want, but not so much you invite your agent to sacrifice your interests to the interests of someone else (including the agent him- or herself).

Mistake No. 83:   *We pushed to get the absolute best deal we could.*

Lesson: The deal's not over till it's over.

"We chose to work with a buyers' agent," recalls Barry Tausch. "We felt a buyers' agent would work harder to get us the best deal possible. As it turned out, though, maybe we pushed too hard.

"We knew the sellers were getting a divorce. The wife had moved out of the house and in with her boss. Without income from the wife's paycheck, the husband was having a tough time keeping up the house payments and supporting their kids. Although they had a lot of equity in the house, the husband was hurting for cash. He really needed a fast sale. By using this information to our advantage, we got the sellers down at least $12,000 or $13,000 below market. Bad deal for them. Good deal for us.

"The only thing we had to agree to was a 30-day close. We didn't think this would be a problem because we already had been prequalified. But it was. There was one foul-up after another.

"In the meantime, the sellers got a backup offer for $7,500 more than our price. To make a long story short, the husband held such resentment against us for 'stealing' his house, he wouldn't cut us any slack. As soon as we missed the close date, he demanded payment. When we couldn't deliver, he pulled out of our contract and sold to the backup buyers."

Negotiating expert Bob Woolf says, "There isn't any contract I have negotiated where I didn't feel I could have gone for more money or an additional benefit." Why? Because skilled negotiators know "the deal's not over till it's over." If you push too hard, you create resentment and hostility in the other party. Even if they've signed a contract, they'll start thinking of all the ways they can get out of it. Even worse, if you stumble on your way to closing, they won't help you up. They'll just kick dirt in your face.

Especially in the purchase of a home—where emotions run strong on both sides—you're usually better off to "leave something on the table." In many instances, the purchase agreement is only stage one of your negotiations. Later problems may pop up with respect to property inspections, the appraisal, financing, possession date, closing date, surveys, or any number of other things. Without goodwill and mutual trust, problems on the way to closing can easily cause an agreement to fall through.

Chapter 7

Arranging Financing

Mistake No. 84: *We had never heard of special financing for people like us.*

Lesson: If you have the will, you can find a way.

"We had always heard that to buy a house you needed 20 percent down and excellent credit," says Rene Wolpe. "Otherwise we would have bought years ago. Until recently, when we learned of Bank of America's Neighborhood Advantage mortgage, we never knew people like us could qualify for special financing."

The Wolpes have made the most common and most costly mistake in real estate. They excluded themselves from home ownership because they falsely believed they couldn't qualify for financing. But as Kathy Ortiz of the San Diego Home Loan Counseling Center points out, "There are a lot of loan programs, and there is a program for almost everyone."

Kathy goes on to say that most of the people she helps are like the Wolpes. They just don't realize how many different ways there are to finance a home. "A large majority of our clients come in here really hesitant and lack the confidence that they can qualify. But when they leave, they leave with confidence because they have developed an understanding of the home-buying process and they know their options."

Javier and Maricela Samaniego are living proof of what Kathy Ortiz is referring to. This young couple with a 16-month-old son never believed they could own their own home. They were paying $550 a month for rent and had meager savings. But thanks to Union Bank's Economic Opportunity Mortgage, they were able to buy. "I thought that without this," says Maricela, "we would have had to come up with more money, and since we didn't have much money to work with, it really helped us a lot. . . . We [now] have so many plans for the house. It really changed everything for us. The money we were paying in rent is now going somewhere."

With the help of Realtors, home builders, mortgage lenders, government agencies, and home counseling centers, hundreds of thousands of Americans like the Wolpes and the Samaniegos are discovering the standard rules of mortgage financing are a relic of the past. Although never etched in stone as many potential homebuyers have believed, in today's push to turn around falling rates of home ownership (especially among minorities and low- to moderate-income individuals and families), nearly every part of the real estate industry is working to make home buying and home financing easier. Although you will need to check your own area to see what's available locally, here's a brief sampling of the types of programs you might turn to.

COMMUNITY REINVESTMENT PROGRAMS

For years civil rights activists and various consumer groups have accused banks and other mortgage lenders of "redlining." According to critics, bank officers take a red marking pen and draw a circle around minority or low- to moderate-income neighborhoods. "These areas are too risky," say the bankers. "We can't finance homes there. Property values may go down."

When bankers do cut off mortgages to an area, they set in motion a self-fulfilling prophecy. If people can't get the money they need to buy and fix up homes in a neighborhood, the neighborhood will decline. But, fortunately, lenders are now recognizing the opposite truth. If they do make loans available, people will invest in their own homes. Neighborhoods will turn around. Values will increase.

So in response to critics, federal antidiscrimination laws, and the profit motive, banks and other mortgage lenders are "rolling out the red carpet" for borrowers who in past years may have been turned away. "We are in a heavy campaign to spread the word to the community that home ownership is not out of reach for low-income families," says mortgage specialist Fred Thomas III. "This is truly a window of opportunity for folks who previously were shut out of the home-buying system."

The specific details of these community reinvestment home finance plans differ among lenders. Some offer low- or no down payment plans. Others eliminate or reduce closing costs and fees. Most relax qualifying standards and offer counseling to help individuals and families shape up their finances, improve their credit, and become familiar with the process of buying a home and the responsibilities of home ownership. A large number of lenders combine all these benefits into one program.

Ray Sims of GE Capital Mortgage Services says of their program, "We expect to create business where we haven't seen it before. . . . We see this as a potentially large underserved market."

Even though community reinvestment loan programs are geared toward "low- to moderate-income" borrowers, the income limits often go up to $40,000, $50,000, or $60,000 a year. Sometimes no limits apply whatsoever. American Savings Bank advertises, "If you pay $1,000 a month or more for rent, you should consider buying a $200,000 house." So don't rule yourself out because you think you earn too much money. Most community reinvestment home finance programs reach well into the middle class.

STATE AND LOCAL GOVERNMENTS

"It's a great program," says Rebecca Hoffreiter. "Anybody that needs it should go for it." Rebecca's talking about a home finance plan sponsored in part by the Pennsylvania Housing Finance Agency (PHFA). Under this innovative lease-purchase plan, renters can move into home ownership with as little as $1,000 in up-front cash. Then for a period of one to three years, a part of the homebuyers' monthly payments go into a forced savings account. Once they build up enough money for a 5 percent down payment, the buyers obtain a mortgage and close on their purchase.

"This is certainly a great program, and we're really excited about it," says Craig Cunningham. Craig is director of marketing for K. Hovnanian, one of the new home builders who has agreed to participate in this lease-purchase program. On the other side of the country, Harry Jensen of Jensen Mortgage says, "We're putting people in $120,000 homes who could have only qualified for a $60,000 home. At the beginning, the Realtors I know were incredulous." Harry's praise is aimed at a shared equity mortgage plan sponsored by the San Diego Housing Commission.

Under this plan, the Housing Commission contributes up to $25,000 in down payment funds. Homebuyers need only come up with 3 percent of the home's purchase price from their own pocket. As an added advantage, the city Housing Commission's down payment money doesn't require any monthly repayments. If the homeowners sell within 15 years, they must then repay the down payment money along with some profit to the Commission. On the other hand, after 15 years the loan is completely forgiven.

Throughout the United States, both state and local governments have created dozens of different types of programs that offer special assistance financing. There are low-interest mortgage bond programs, mortgage credit certificates, low-cost home repair or renovation loans, down payment assistance plans, and even sweat equity and urban homesteading. Some states have also created their own version of the VA (U.S. Department of Veterans Affairs) mortgages.

WHERE TO LOOK

Locating a community reinvestment mortgage or other special assistance finance plan that's right for you takes some work. You may need to talk to Realtors, loan officers, mortgage brokers, government agencies, and home-buying counselors. It also helps to read the business and real estate sections of the major newspapers in your city or state. But if you stay alert and persevere, you can find a home finance plan with your name on it.

Mistake No. 85:   *We thought FHA only loaned to low-income people and involved too much red tape.*

Lesson: *Don't overlook loans insured by the Federal Housing Administration.*

"We earn $48,000 a year," says Sam Wright. "We didn't know we could get an FHA loan since we fall well outside the low-income category. Anyway, whenever you get involved with the government, you've got too much red tape to wade through."

Sam has made a common mistake. Many Americans erroneously believe FHA mortgage loan programs are intended only for low- to moderate-income individuals and families. In fact, FHA places no limits on income. It doesn't matter whether you earn $12,000 a year or $120,000; as long as you've got acceptable (not perfect) credit and earn enough to make your mortgage payments, you can qualify. As to red tape, the FHA does have its bureaucratic rules and regulations. But these shouldn't present a problem for borrowers who are working with a DE (direct endorsement) lender. These lenders can complete and approve the loan paperwork directly, without submitting it to the FHA.

Compared to most conventional home mortgages, FHA home finance plans have only two disadvantages. In areas of the country with high house prices, FHA loan limits may be too low. In California, for example, median home prices run around $200,000, but the current FHA maximum loan amount is around $150,000. In more moderately priced areas of the country, though, typical FHA loan limits of $75,000 to $110,000 can adequately cover the price of most starter homes. Even in high-priced cities such as Los Angeles, San Francisco, Washington, D.C., and Boston, FHA loans often can work well for condominiums, townhouses, and lower-priced neighborhoods.

The second disadvantage of FHA loans is cost. Compared to many private mortgages, FHA mortgage insurance and fees can add an extra $1,000 to $2,500 to your closing expenses. To offset these higher expenses, though, the FHA does let you roll most of the costs into your loan. You don't have to pay much at closing.

Overall, in deciding whether to choose an FHA loan, you need to weigh its disadvantages against these benefits:

- Low down payment—usually 5 percent or less.
- Easier qualifying. FHA lenders often will not be as picky as conventional lenders. The primary purpose of FHA is to expand home ownership. FHA lenders can't broaden home ownership by turning down people who want to buy homes.
- More liberal qualifying ratios. This means FHA may qualify you for a larger loan than will most conventional lenders.
- HUD/FHA offers homebuyer and homeowner counseling through hundreds of not-for-profit organizations located throughout the country. These counselors can tell you what you need to do to become a homeowner. And should you suffer a layoff, health problem, or other financial setback after you've bought your home,

FHA counselors can reduce your mortgage payments and help you sort through and solve your budget problems.

- If you finance your home with an FHA loan and mortgage interest rates drop, you can "streamline" an FHA refinance to take advantage of the lower rates. Streamlining means you don't have to jump over any qualifying hurdles again. There's no credit check, no income verification, no appraisal, no points. No conventional lender offers this super deal.

- When you sell your home, your buyers can, upon qualifying, assume your FHA fixed-rate mortgage at the same rate you're paying. If interest rates fall, they too will be able to streamline a refinance at the new lower rates.

These last two features, streamlining and assumability, are great FHA benefits. In recent years as economic hard times have hit some homeowners, they haven't been able to refinance their conventional loans because their income, their home's value, or both have fallen. They've been stuck with old mortgages of 10 to 13 percent even as market rates hovered around 7 percent. In contrast, through streamlining a refinance, FHA borrowers have been able to cut their mortgage payments by hundreds of dollars a month—even when they could not have qualified for new financing.

As an additional advantage, FHA assumability will give you a competitive edge over other sellers when you put your home up for sale. If interest rates are high, you can pass along your lower rate to buyers. If market interest rates have fallen, you or your buyers can streamline a refinance. Your buyers prevent the hassle and cost of taking out a new loan. In addition, qualifying for an FHA assumption is usually easier than qualifying for a new loan.

All in all, I believe the benefits of FHA greatly outweigh its disadvantages. Although only you can decide what's best for your circumstances, don't make the mistake of overlooking FHA. During the past five years FHA has helped more than 3.5 million Americans become homeowners. This is one government agency that must be doing something right.

Mistake No. 86:   *We wanted a fixed-rate mortgage. ARMs were too risky.*

Lesson: *Before you pass up an ARM, make sure you understand and explore your options.*

"When we started shopping for a home," recalls Ari Kyle, "I read that you should avoid an ARM whenever you can get a 30-year fixed-rate mortgage for less than 10 percent. Since at the time, 30-year mortgages were fluctuating around 8 percent, we didn't even consider an adjustable rate. With fixed rates that low, why take the risk of an ARM?"

Although Ari asked this question rhetorically, the answer is not as obvious as he thinks. In fact, like Ari, far too many homebuyers pass up ARMs without fully considering why some type of adjustable-rate mortgage might prove to be their best choice. Before you make this mistake, give yourself this little quiz:

1.   Is there a strong probability you will sell your home within seven years?

2.   Do you expect your income to increase during the coming years?

3.   Would you like to increase your home purchase price range by $10,000 to $40,000, or even more?

4.   Would you like to cut your closing costs by $1,000 to $3,000?

5.   Do you expect to keep your home for more than seven years?

If you can answer yes to at least two of these five questions, you should fully explore your ARM options.

First, the shorter the length of time you plan to own your home, the more you should consider an ARM. That's because nearly all ARMs place a ceiling on how high your monthly payments can climb. As a rule, you can nearly always find an adjustable that will cost you less than a fixed-rate loan if you plan to sell within seven years. As a minimum, take a look at 5/25 or 7/23 (sometimes described as a 30/5 or 30/7) adjustable.

These types of ARMs fix your interest rate and monthly payments for the beginning five or seven years of the loan. Then they periodically adjust to keep your rate in line with the market. Even this limited type of adjustable may save you between .5 and 1.5 percent in interest as compared to a fixed-rate mortgage. For instance, when 30-year fixed-rates were at 7.25 percent, I saw several 5/25 ARM plans with interest rates as low as 5.75 percent.

On a $100,000 loan, your payments for a 7.25 percent 30-year fixed-rate loan would run $682 a month. If you selected the 5/25, your payments would drop to $583. Although the precise cost differences between 30-year fixed-rate loans and various types of ARMs change daily, it pays to explore the market. When you plan to sell within seven years, the chances are good you can find an ARM that limits your risk at the same time it reduces your monthly payments. You have the best of both worlds.

On top of this, if you're fairly certain your income is going up over the coming years, you should be able to handle any increases in your ARM's monthly payments. Take a careful look at your future expenses and factor in salary raises. Do you have some breathing room? If you do, don't needlessly worry about an adjustable-rate mortgage (as long as its payment increases are moderately capped, of course).

As an additional advantage, ARMs help you qualify for a larger mortgage. They do this in two ways. First, since ARMs start with lower interest rates, for the same amount of monthly payment, you can borrow more. A payment of say $800 a month will pay off a loan of $109,000 at 8 percent over 30 years. With an ARM's qualifying interest rate of 6 percent, you could borrow $133,000. Second, even better, if you can afford it, some ARM lenders will qualify you with more liberal qualifying ratios. For example, with a fixed-rate loan, the lender might limit your payments to $800 a month. But with an ARM, the lender might qualify you for a monthly payment of, say, $840. Instead of borrowing $109,000 (with an 8 percent fixed-rate loan), the 6 percent ARM with liberal qualifying would permit you to borrow $140,000.

To further encourage you to use an ARM, many lenders cut their loan origination fees and closing costs. This benefit, however, may not be the advantage it once was. To meet competitive pressures, some lenders also have been offering low cash-to-close deals on their fixed-rate loans. Nevertheless, don't forget to at least compare adjustable- and fixed-rate mortgages on the basis of cash you need to close.

Now nearly all experts agree that ARMs may save you money if you plan to sell within seven years or less. But you also might save money over the longer term. Here's why.

Say you're faced with a choice between a 30-year fixed-rate loan at 8 percent and a 7/23 that starts at 6.75 percent. You want to borrow $100,000. With the fixed-rate plan, your payments will run $733 a month. With the 7/23, you'll pay $648. So for at least the first seven years, you'll save $85 a month, for a total of $7,140.

Instead of pocketing this $85 a month, though, let's assume you add it to your mortgage payment. Even though you're only required to pay $648, you go ahead and pay $733. This tactic causes you to pay down your mortgage balance much faster. If you did that, your outstanding mortgage balance after seven years would have fallen to approximately $83,000. On the other hand, your balance with the fixed-rate plan at 8 percent would have dropped to just $92,480. Obviously, if you sell at this point, you're way ahead of the game with the ARM.

But what if you don't want to sell? As long as your new rate stays below 9.5 percent, your monthly mortgage payments won't amount to any more than $740—about the same as you've been paying. At 10.5 percent, your payments would increase only to $798 a month. Now, what if interest rates have remained about the same or fallen? Not only will you have accumulated an additional $9,480 in home equity, but your monthly payments won't increase and may actually go down.

Of course, these figures are illustrative only. Because the relative costs of ARMs versus fixed-rate loans change frequently, you'll have to work the numbers with your mortgage loan advisor that are current at the time you buy your home. Nevertheless, the basic idea holds true. For some homebuyers, the right ARM can put them thousands of dollars ahead of where they would have been with a fixed-rate mortgage.

By pointing out many of the potential advantages of ARMs, I don't mean to imply they're right for everyone. In fact, some homebuyers choose ARMs when they should stick with fixed-rate mortgages. On the other hand, don't needlessly fear ARMs because they're "too risky." Think through the benefits. Compare costs. Look for ways to limit risk through annual caps and/or longer-term adjustment periods. You might find an ARM is your best choice after all.

Mistake No. 87:   *We didn't think to negotiate for seller financing.*

Lesson: *Even when you believe you'll qualify for financing from a bank or savings institution, don't ignore the possibility of seller financing.*

Like many homebuyers, Julio and Tara Scott only had enough cash for a 10 percent down payment. So when they bought their home, their bank charged them a higher interest rate and required them to purchase private mortgage insurance (PMI). In addition, because the mortgage insurer applied tight qualifying standards, the Scotts weren't able to buy as much house as they wanted. In other words, the Scotts ended up paying more and getting less.

What the Scotts overlooked was a financing method referred to as an 80-10-10 sale. This technique works like this: You put 10 percent down; you borrow 80 percent of your home's purchase price from a bank or S&L; and the sellers carry back the other 10 percent as a seller-financed second mortgage.

Since under this plan the bank has made an 80 percent loan instead of a 90 percent loan, it faces less risk. In exchange for this lower risk, the bank will drop its requirements for PMI, give you a better interest rate, and probably relax its qualifying income ratios or other credit standards. You can get more house for less.

Now, you might ask, "What's in it for the sellers? Why would they accept this kind of deal?"

Most important, the sellers get their house sold. For most sellers, that's their number-one priority. When you write up your offer, you make an 80-10-10 plan a condition of the contract. Second, because it's easier to qualify at the bank for an 80 percent loan, the sellers can feel a little more secure your purchase will actually close. Many sellers fear they will pull their house off the market for four to eight weeks, then their sale falls through, and they're back at square one. Anything you do to reduce this fear stands out as a plus in the sellers' eyes.

Third, the interest you agree to pay the sellers will exceed the amount they could earn on their money in a certificate of deposit or savings account. With CDs paying 3 or 4 percent, a return of 7 to 9 percent to the sellers on a second mortgage can look pretty good. Fourth, an 80-10-10 sale will probably take less time to close than a 90-10 sale with private mortgage insurance.

OTHER VARIATIONS

Of course, an 80-10-10 sale represents just one variation of combined seller-bank financing. If you're really short of cash, you could try for an 80-15-5 plan, or even an 80-20-0. In fact, any combination is possible. If your credit has some blemishes, you could decrease the bank's percentage to 60 to 75 percent—say 70-20-10. Just remember: The lower the bank's loan-to-value ratio, the greater your chance for loan approval, the less likely you'll have to buy PMI, and the lower your interest rate.

ELIMINATE THE BANK ALTOGETHER

Homebuyers who can't qualify for bank financing know they must turn to some type of seller financing or nonqualifying mortgage assumption. But even when you do think you can bank qualify, you still might consider negotiating a completely seller-financed purchase. Here are some reasons why seller financing is beneficial.

- Often you can get the sellers to accept a lower interest rate than the bank.
- Sellers don't often charge application fees, "garbage" fees, or loan origination fees. You need less cash to close.
- Seller financing involves less paperwork and a quicker closing.
- You can tailor the exact terms, amounts, and payment schedule to you and the sellers' needs. You don't have to get stuck in the red tape of government rules and regulations.

More than 40 percent of the homeowners in the United States and Canada own their homes free and clear. These homeowners are prime candidates to carry back all or a substantial part of your financing. Yet sometimes you have to do more than ask. You have to make seller financing an essential condition of your purchase offer. Then itemize and explain the benefits. If you make your offer reasonable and responsive to the sellers' needs, you'll find many can be persuaded to accept.

Mistake No. 88:   *Those were the fastest two years of our lives.*

Lesson: *Beware of home financing that falls due in less time than it takes to wear out a pair of shoes.*

"We never worried about it at the time," says Ruth Redkey. "We were sure interest rates would come down and our home would appreciate. We couldn't imagine any trouble refinancing. But interest rates didn't

---

come down. Our home didn't appreciate. And those were the fastest two years of our lives."

When Ruth and her boyfriend, Sid, bought their home, they used a 70-20-10 financing plan. They borrowed 70 percent of their home's price from the bank; the sellers financed 20 percent; and Ruth and Sid put up 10 percent as a down payment. This technique made it easier for the couple to qualify for bank financing and it saved them money. Not only did the bank give them a lower interest rate, the sellers even agreed to accept an interest rate less than the bank was charging. But here's the catch: Ruth and Sid agreed to pay off the sellers' loan within two years. And they couldn't do it.

Ruth and Sid had fallen into a common trap. Sometimes sellers who carry back financing will grant their buyers very favorable terms for a year or two. After this relatively short term, the seller financing falls due. The buyers then have to either come up with the money themselves or arrange new financing.

Although in and of itself, there's nothing inherently wrong with short-term financing, it does present risks that too many homebuyers ignore. Ruth says, "We were so eager to stop throwing rent money down a rat hole, we were willing to accept almost any terms the seller wanted. Back then two years seemed like a long time. With the prospects of home ownership so close, we shut our mind to the risks. As far as we were concerned, there weren't any. We told each other interest rates had to come down. We told each other our home would probably go up in value by at least 10 to 15 percent. Talking between ourselves was like talking in an echo chamber. Neither of us critically listened. We just repeated what the other one said."

Sid and Ruth's sleepless nights and anxious days demonstrate the risks of short-term financing. Over a period of one to three years, no one can accurately predict interest rates or home appreciation rates. Although it's often easy to tell yourself you'll be able to refinance, experience too often has proven otherwise.

In fact, as many Southern Californians and New Englanders learned in the late 1980s and early 1990s, over the short term home values can fall even when interest rates have hit their lowest levels since automobile tailfins were popular. Many of these homeowners couldn't refinance their short-term seller carrybacks. Although a new loan would have meant lower payments, their home values would no longer support the amount of mortgage they needed.

To prevent getting caught in refinance limbo:

- Insist on a payoff date no earlier than five to seven years. Don't risk short-term future shock for the immediate joy of home ownership.
- If you do agree to a shorter-term loan, include an escape clause that extends your due date if home values are depressed or if interest rates have risen.
- As an additional safeguard, develop a plan to create value. Shorter-term finance plans work best when you buy a home at a bargain price. Then redecorate, remodel, or renovate to boost its loan value (or future selling price).

SPECIAL NOTE ON LEASE-OPTIONS

One of the most popular short-term seller finance plans is the lease-option. Most lease-option agreements call for buyers to execute their option to buy within one to two years. Usually buyers use this time to save money for a down payment, strengthen their credit record, or pay off some of their other bills. For tens of thousands of former renters, the lease-option has been their admission ticket to home ownership.

If you do choose a lease-option home finance plan, however, remember you face the risk that interest rates will go up before you're able to buy. So, just as with short-term mortgages, try to protect your position. Write a clause into your agreement that gives you more time to close if interest rates head north. You would want to follow this advice especially if you're paying substantially more for your option and lease payments than you would be paying in straight rent for another similar home. Don't leave yourself wide open to the danger that you won't qualify for the financing (refinancing) you need.

Mistake No. 89:   *I paid $2,500 down to lease-option a townhouse but then found out later that my bank wouldn't give me a mortgage on it.*

Lesson: *Not all properties or "down payments" meet lender rules and regulations.*

Like many tenants, Eric Coffey was tired of wasting money on rent. But financially, he wasn't quite ready to buy. Eric wanted time to pay off his car loan, cut down his credit card debt, and build up more savings for a down payment and cash reserves. So Eric decided to look for a seller who would give him a lease-option.

"After just three weeks of searching," recalls Eric, "I felt real lucky because I found just what I wanted. It was a large end-unit townhouse with two bedrooms, two and a half baths, fireplace, and a lower-level study. At $129,500 it was priced right, and the seller agreed to an eighteen-month lease-option. Our terms looked like this: I paid $2,500 to move in; my monthly rent payment was $1,200; and out of that $1,200, I received a rent credit toward the purchase price of $500 a month.

"I was quite pleased with this arrangement," Eric continued. "Everything went well for the first 16 months. Altogether, I had accumulated $18,000 toward my down payment and cash reserves. I had the option payment of $2,500, rent credits of $9,000, and additional savings of $6,500. That was more than enough for a 10 percent down payment and closing costs. I had even paid down my bills like I planned.

"But my bank still turned down my loan application. The loan officer said too many homeowners in the complex were renting out their townhouses instead of living there themselves. To further complicate matters, the bank would not count my rent credits as part of my down payment. Here I was: I'd been doing business with this bank for eight years. I had never made a late payment on my car loan or bounced a check. Yet the lender wouldn't make me the mortgage. I began to panic that I was going to lose the townhouse and all the money I'd put into it.

"In the end we did get things worked out. The bank made a 70 percent loan, the seller carried back 20 percent, and I contributed my 10 percent. But it was really touch and go for a while."

When Eric entered into his lease-option agreement, he had mistakenly overlooked the fact that many lenders won't give mortgages for condo and townhouse complexes with high numbers of renters. Once a complex drops to less than 60 or 70 percent owner occupancy, lenders believe values in the complex may start to decline. When a project "tips" too much toward rentals, upkeep and maintenance often deteriorate.

Eric also faced a second problem. Some lenders are suspect of "funny money" down payments. They prefer cash down from your bank account. If instead you want to use your car, a stamp collection, or rent credits as part of your down payment, the lender may feel you and the sellers are manipulating the numbers. In the past, many lease-option sellers have simply overpriced the homes they were selling. In exchange, they give buyers a large rent credit so it appears like they're building equity—at least on paper. But in fact the rent credit is just whittling down the price to where it should have been to begin with.

Say you agree to pay $110,000 for a condo (or house) that's actually valued at $100,000. Over two years you build up $11,000 in rent credits that you want to count as a down payment. From the lender's viewpoint, those rent credits are "funny money." Even after counting them against your purchase price, you'll still owe just about what the home is worth. So the lender says no deal. You've got to come up with a lot more real cash.

The solution to both these problems is first to avoid condo or townhouse developments that are close to tipping toward renters. (This is good advice regardless of whether you're using a lease-option.) And second, make sure your option terms can pass a lender's sniff test. If your agreement doesn't smell right, the lender probably won't go for it. The lender will try to make sure your rent levels, rent credits, and purchase price make sense in terms of the market. A lender doesn't want to make a 80 or 90 percent loan-to-value ratio loan that actually turns out to be a 95 or 100 percent loan.

Mistake No. 90: *We paid too much for our mortgage. We didn't question our agent's referral.*

Lesson: *Don't accept your agent's (or home builder's) mortgage referral without comparison shopping.*

Until 1993, some real estate agents routinely received kickbacks from mortgage lenders. Although RESPA (the Real Estate Settlement and Procedures Act) supposedly outlawed this practice, it was common in many cities throughout the United States for some lenders to pay agents under-the-table referral fees. In fact, sometimes unethical agents even *demanded* that lenders pay them kickbacks for bringing in loan customers.

Beth and Ted Cippolla were one couple who fell victim to such an agent. "We trusted him," says Beth. "He told us we didn't need to waste time calling a dozen lenders because he had a special arrangement with a mortgage company who would give his buyers the best mortgage terms possible. Sure, he had a special arrangement all right. But the arrangement wasn't to get us the best deal. It was to get Harold [their agent] a free trip to Hawaii. It cost us an extra $900 in closing costs and one-quarter percent on our mortgage interest rate."

In an effort to stamp out abuses like the Cippollas suffered, the U.S. Department of Housing and Urban Development (HUD) has cracked down on illegal kickbacks and referral fees. In several well-publicized court cases, HUD has gone after offenders with civil fines and criminal prosecutions. In addition, HUD has strengthened its rules and regulations. "Under current law," says HUD division director David Williamson, "if agents aren't providing a bona fide financial service, they aren't entitled to a referral fee or any other kind of extra compensation or anything of value."

However, what HUD has taken away with its left hand, it has given back double with its right hand. Under HUD's new rules, agents may not lawfully accept under-the-table referral fees; but they can now act as fully authorized loan originators. In other words, real estate brokerage firms have been given the green light to compete directly with lenders, mortgage brokers, and mortgage bankers. In fact, some of the larger realty firms have even bought or set up their own mortgage companies. When a realty firm actually provides mortgage services (not just referrals), it can legally charge buyers (borrowers) for these services.

These regulations and changes are too new to tell whether homebuyers will gain or lose from them. HUD and the National Association of Realtors maintain consumers will benefit. They say as long as real estate agents follow the law and fully disclose all fees, homebuyers will enjoy a greater choice of mortgages.

The Mortgage Bankers Association, though, sees realty firms invading their turf and doesn't like it. The mortgage bankers say the new rules will reduce competition. Agents will steer homebuyers—and especially first-time homebuyers—to lenders who are affiliated with the realty firms. And there's no guarantee those lenders will actually offer borrowers the best terms or interest rates. Stephen Brobeck, who's with the Consumer Federation of America, agrees with the mortgage bankers. This group has gone on record to oppose HUD and the Realtors.

In response, Realtors have countered that they would be foolish to steer their buyers to uncompetitive loan products or mortgage lenders. It wouldn't take long for word to get out and that realty firm would lose not only its mortgage business, it would lose real estate sales.

"Consumers have never been shy to squeal when they are not satisfied," says Realtor spokeswoman Sally Sciacca.

As the debate stands now, I believe HUD and the Realtors have put forward the best arguments. Still, as in any field, some real estate agents will abuse their trust. So become a savvy borrower. Don't accept your real estate agent's loan products without first checking the rates, terms, and qualifying standards of other lenders. HUD's new rules can work well only if you don't forget to think for yourself. Count on your real estate agent to advise and suggest. But remember, it's up to you to make an informed choice.

Mistake No. 91:   *Our lender rejected our loan approval because I went into labor early and had to take temporary disability.*

Lesson: *If you change your* loan status *before you close your mortgage, your lender may revoke your approval.*

Kristi Colburn and her husband, Pat, did all the right things to buy their home. They saved diligently. They ran up no large debts. They kept their credit record spotless. They both worked steadily since graduating from college seven years earlier. And before they started their home search, they received a preapproval (not merely a prequalification) of their loan application. (A prequalification tells you how much house you can probably afford according to the lender's standards. With a preapproval, the lender moves to the next step and actually commits to making you a loan.)

"Everything was going great," says Kristi. "We found a terrific three-bedroom, two and one-half bath in Brighton less than 15 minutes from work for both of us. Our offer was accepted and we went into escrow. After years of waiting and months of searching, we were just two weeks away from becoming homeowners. Our loan officer told us from now until closing would be smooth sailing. Just paperwork formalities—nothing to be concerned about.

"Instead of smooth sailing, though, during the next two weeks, our sailing ship lost its wind and we hit choppy seas," recalls Kristi. "Eight months along in my pregnancy, I started to feel severe labor pains. It became too difficult for me to work, so I went on disability leave. Ten days later I delivered our daughter Jessy—as healthy and strong as a baby can be.

"But at the same time we gained a daughter, we lost our loan. The day after I got home from the hospital, the loan officer called and said I needed to go back to my job immediately or the lender would refuse to close the loan. The mortgage approval was conditioned upon both our incomes, he said. Of course, we knew that and I did intend to return to work—but not for two or three months. The loan officer replied that wasn't good enough. He said I had to go back now.

"In trying to find a satisfactory solution, over the next six weeks we went through sheer agony. Our apartment lease expired and we had to move in with Pat's parents. My mom agreed to cosign our note. My employer assured the lender my job was waiting for me any time I was ready to end my maternity leave. We increased our down payment to 20 percent. The lender switched us from the fixed-rate loan we wanted to an ARM.

"Each time we would make one of these concessions or accept a new lender demand, the loan officer would reschedule our closing date. Then he would call and cancel until we agreed to something else. It was ridiculous.

"But you won't believe what happened next," Kristi added. "After meeting all the lender's additional requirements, and suffering through three cancellations and reschedulings, the loan officer informed us the loan committee had once again changed its decision. If we wanted the loan, I would still have to go back to work immediately, receive a paycheck, and then show the lender my paystub.

"At that point, we were totally frustrated and exhausted. There was nothing we could do. We needed a home and weren't about to start looking for another apartment to rent. So I had no choice. I went back to work, got my paystub, and finally, escrow closed."

Your first reaction to Kristi's ordeal might be that the lender discriminated against Kristi because of her pregnancy and the birth of her daughter. But no matter how absurdly the lender handled Kristi and Pat Colburn's loan processing, it acted within its rights. Whenever a mortgage applicant changes his or her *loan status* prior to closing, the lender can revoke its loan approval. Since technically Kristi's job income had stopped, the lender wasn't required to count it. Without the income, the Colburns no longer qualified. Not fair or reasonable. But it is the law.

Now in Kristi's case, her loss of income (even if temporary) triggered the change in the Colburns' loan status. However, all the factors a lender considers in its loan decision will actually contribute to your loan status:

- Income
- Other bills, debts, and expenses
- Length of employment
- Job security
- Credit record
- Available cash
- Net worth
- Type of loan, interest rate, amount of your scheduled payments including property taxes, homeowners' insurance, and mortgage insurance (if any)

Upon learning that their mortgage had been approved, Phil and Sue Grubbs went out and charged $3,000 of new furniture for their home. When the lender learned of these additional bills through a last-minute credit reverification, the Grubbs lost their mortgage approval. Their additional bills knocked them out of qualifying. Jack Reeves was preapproved for his home loan and then accepted a better job at higher pay. Thinking this was good news, Jack told his loan officer. The loan officer revoked Jack's preapproved commitment. The lender thought new jobs were too insecure. "Come back after a year," the loan officer told Jack.

When it comes to approving and closing loans, lenders show a split personality. Sometimes they will lean over backward to bend the rules to get a borrower qualified. On other occasions they act as if they've locked their common sense in one of their money vaults. So a word to the wise: After you've applied for a loan, don't do anything that can adversely change your loan status. If you do, your lender may give you the same kind of hassle (or rejection) that hit the Colburns, Grubbs, and Reeves.

Mistake No. 92:   *My loan fell through because of poor credit. But it wasn't my credit that was bad.*

Lesson: *Get your credit record and finances in shape before you begin to shop for your home.*

Gwen Davis knew she had excellent credit and had never made a late payment in her life. So she didn't bother reviewing her credit report

---

before she began shopping for a home. As Gwen now realizes, that shortcut proved to be a mistake. It cost her the home she wanted.

"I couldn't believe it," says Gwen. "I was in shock. The loan officer told me the credit report showed I was two months behind on my car loan and that my Visa card had been canceled for nonpayment. 'I don't even have a car loan,' I told him. 'Look on my mortgage application. Or I can show you the title to my car.'

"The loan officer sympathized with me but said his hands were tied. If the credit report erred, it would be up to me to straighten it out. Until I could show him a clean record, my application would not even be considered.

"My next step," Gwen continued, "was to try to get to the bottom of this. So I went to the credit bureau and got a copy of my credit report. Sure enough, the black marks were there for all the world to see. But as I knew, they didn't belong in my file. What had happened was the credit bureau had mingled my record with the record of Gail Davis—my ex-husband's new wife.

"At this point, my education of the credit bureaucracy was just beginning. I soon learned discovering a problem is one thing. Fixing it is something else. To get those black marks off my record required endless phone calls, a dozen letters, and threats from my attorney. To make matters worse, Gail didn't lift a finger to help. She wasn't eager to see delinquent accounts reappear in her file. All told, it took four months to clear my name. By then the sellers had already sold their home to other buyers. I really wanted that house too."

You can prevent Gwen's mistake by contacting your local credit bureau or one of the national credit repositories (TRW, TransUnion, Equifax). Ask them to provide you a copy of your credit report. (They may charge a small fee.) Then examine the report carefully. If you discover bad credit that doesn't belong to you, tell the credit bureau. Immediately do what's necessary to get it removed. As Gwen Davis found out, that process can sometimes take months.

On the other hand, if you find some late payments or other blemishes that are yours, realize that these may stop many lenders from granting you a mortgage. As a minimum, you must make sure all your installment accounts are current. Should you have any outstanding past-due debts, judgments, or tax liens, you will need to pay them. Very few mortgage lenders will loan money to someone who has not paid money that is legally owed. This practice even extends to disputed claims. The lender won't take your word. By whatever means you can, you will have to clear them from your record. You will have to negotiate, litigate, or otherwise satisfy the claims.

Since the S&L debacle of the 1980s, the great majority of financial institutions only want borrowers who have maintained near-perfect credit records for at least the past 12 to 24 months. The lenders might forgive a late payment or two, if you write a satisfactory explanation. But anything more than a few minor blemishes will invite a turndown.

The best way then to guard against a turndown is to review your credit record, get your finances in the best shape you can, and search for the right lender and loan product for your situation. Getting approval for home financing is like a matching contest. You have to figure your strengths and weaknesses. Then before you formally apply, try to identify the lender(s) whose qualifying criteria best fits your borrower profile. Otherwise you're flying blind.

Mistake No. 93:   *The lender's appraiser lowballed us.*

Lesson: *You have a right to examine and question your lender's appraisal.*

"We had spent almost a year looking at houses," says Phil Tortellori. "We liked a lot of them, but for one reason or other nothing quite excited our fancy. Then one Saturday afternoon by accident we drove by a house we knew we had to have. Best of all, it was priced right—or I should say, we thought it was priced right. Unfortunately, less than 10 days before closing, we learned the lender's appraiser had reported a different opinion. Her estimate of the home's value came in $10,000 less than our purchase price.

"To offset this lower appraised value, the lender said we'd have to increase our down payment by $8,000. Or, instead, we could ask the sellers to reduce their price. We had bargained hard as it was, so we didn't think the sellers would agree to come down more. And they wouldn't. As for raising our down payment by $8,000, no way could we do that. So, the financing fell through and we had to begin our home search all over again."

Home financing experiences like Phil Tortellori's became increasingly common throughout the early 1990s. Both homebuyers and home sellers have complained of lowball appraisals that killed home sales. In some instances lenders have used low appraisals to turn down loans they didn't want to make. At other times lenders or their appraisers have given low appraisals in reaction to tightened government appraisal regulations. Either way, a lowball appraisal can definitely spoil your home-buying plans.

To help prevent this problem, you can do several different things: First, before you offer to buy a home, make sure your agent shows you recent sales prices (and terms) of similar homes in the neighborhood. Use those prices as a guide for your purchase offer. Second, if possible, learn the name of the appraiser your lender plans to use. Have your agent tell the appraiser the comp sales you relied on to figure your offer. Third, once the appraisal is complete, get a copy from the lender. (You are entitled to a copy of your appraisal under the 1991 Equal Credit Opportunity Act as well as various state laws and the rules and regulations of the Federal Reserve Board.) Examine the appraisal according to the checks we discussed in Chapter 3. Does the appraiser's estimate of value match or exceed your purchase price? If so, great.

If not, you have to decide whether you still want to go through with your purchase. If your lender doesn't approve your loan because of the appraisal, you can legitimately back out of the transaction and recover your earnest money deposit. On the other hand, if you think the appraiser has lowballed you, schedule a meeting with the appraiser, or write out your objections to the appraisal and give them to your lender.

In response, the appraiser can either accept or reject your comments. If he or she rejects them, you can ask the lender to send out another appraiser. If the lender wants your business, it will probably agree to obtain a second opinion. But if the lender doesn't oblige, you will have to ask the sellers to reduce their price, increase your down payment, or apply for your mortgage somewhere else. (To appease your frustrations with the appraiser, you could write a complaint to the state licensing board. But that won't help you get the financing you need.)

By early 1994 most real estate markets around the country had perked up and lowballing no longer posed as large a problem as it once did. Still, it's a practice you need to stay alert for. Lenders do tend to exercise more caution in down markets (early 1990s) than in boom markets (mid- to late 1980s). On the other hand, in sharply rising markets—at least in the past—you have to watch out for "overappraising." With rapid rates of appreciation, lenders, appraisers, and homebuyers alike can get careless. With eyes focused on the future, no one worries much about the price today, because it's sure to be even higher tomorrow.

Regardless, though, of the type of market you're in, don't accept your lender's appraisal without careful examination. To protect your interests, you have a right to question (and challenge) the appraiser's opinion. (Of course, after you see the appraisal, you also might want to reconsider your own estimate of the home's value.)

As a last remark on appraisals, keep in mind one more thing. Appraisers limit their value estimates to the house and lot (real estate). If your purchase agreement includes any expensive personal property (antique Oriental rugs, custom-made draperies, furniture), or if the seller is paying all or a large part of your mortgage points and closing costs, the lender's appraiser can legitimately exclude these amounts from his or her value estimate. In cases like this, there's a good chance you won't be able to borrow the full 80, 90, or 95 percent of your purchase price. So before you write seller concessions directly into your contract, learn your lender's rules on concessions and ask your real estate agent (or attorney) to figure out the best way to handle them. Sometimes it's to your advantage to write up a separate agreement to cover these items.

Chapter 8

Becoming a Homeowner

Mistake No. 94: *Our friends told us we were getting a great deal.*

Lesson: *Be careful how you interpret the advice of friends, relatives, real estate agents, and attorneys.*

Bruce Carver was both anxious and enthusiastic about becoming a homeowner. So after finding the home he wanted to own, Bruce enlisted several of his friends to come over and take a look at the house he had selected. "This is great," they told him. "You're really getting a good buy." Of course these words of encouragement were exactly what Bruce wanted to hear. Bruce wasn't actually seeking an honest opinion. More than anything, he wanted support for a decision he had already made.

Bruce had fallen in love with the home's rear deck and canyon views. He didn't want to hear about the small size of the home's bedrooms, its lack of closet and storage space, or the home's many needed repairs, which included an aging and leaky roof. Sensing Bruce's enthusiasm, his friends avoided giving him the advice he really needed. Nevertheless, Bruce used the opinions they did offer to calm the anxieties about the home's problems that lurked in the back of his mind.

Bruce bought the house, but high costs of repairs and cramped living conditions soon dampened his enchantment with his deck and canyon views. Bruce admitted that he believed he had made a mistake. Along with being captivated by the home's desirable features, Bruce had misinterpreted and misused the advice he had sought.

Naturally, like Bruce, when you buy a home you'll turn to advice from friends, relatives, your real estate agent, and maybe an attorney. But before you interpret and rely on this advice, ask yourself these questions.

Do I really want critical counsel? Or do I want someone who simply agrees with me? There's an old saying among consultants and research analysts that most clients want to use advice like a drunk uses a lamppost—for support, not for illumination. If support is what you really want, your friends will probably oblige. But if that's the case, make sure you recognize such advice for what it is.

Do the people I'm asking for advice really have the information, experience, and expertise necessary to tell me what I need to know? Unless your friends or relatives have recently been shopping for a home in the same neighborhood where you've been looking, they probably can't tell you accurately whether you're getting a good buy. If your lawyer sister hasn't seen a real estate contract since her Real Property I course in law school, chances are she's not the attorney who should review your home purchase agreement.

You may be working with one of the best real estate agents in the state. But if your home tour takes you into neighborhoods or communities where your agent can't find her way without constantly studying a map, it's probably time to bring in another agent who's more familiar with the area. Whether friend, relative, lawyer, or sales agent, just because someone is willing to offer an opinion doesn't mean he or she actually knows enough to give you the advice you need.

Do my advisors really understand my needs and goals? Or are they applying their own preferences or standards? Here's an area where nearly all of us could do better. Often when we ask for advice, we don't really explain our needs, goals, or the most important things we're trying to achieve. Sometimes we don't even know ourselves. On the other hand, when we offer counsel, it's just as likely we will shade our advice toward our own biases, preferences, and standards. We won't (or can't) see the other person's perspective.

If you ask your brother to tell you what he thinks of that darling three-bedroom ranch in Windsor Heights, he could answer, "What? That dump. I wouldn't even think about living in that house or neighborhood." Now, has your brother answered in the context of your needs? Or does he have some personal bias against ranch-style homes or Windsor Heights? What if your agent tells you Troy Woods is not a good area? Should you accept that advice at face value? Or should you question why the agent holds that view? Maybe the agent doesn't like Troy Woods because he doesn't think much of its schools. But if you don't have kids or you're planning to send your kids to a private school, the reasons for your agent's objections might even work to your advantage. Maybe with less attractive schools, homes in Troy Woods provide more house for the money. Rather than being helpful, your agent's (or brother's) advice could actually work against your most important needs.

If people don't understand what you want, or if they can't put aside their own biases, you probably shouldn't pay much attention to their advice.

Do your advisors' interests conflict with your own? Whenever you're interpreting or relying on the advice of other people, keep in mind the fact that their interests may conflict with yours. Some unethical real estate agents may try to talk you into a house (or financing) that doesn't meet your needs just so they can gain a commission. Your parents may talk against an outlying neighborhood because they'd rather see you live closer to them. Your friends could advise you not to buy a home because they're jealous; or maybe they think that if you move you will drift apart as friends.

Everyone has their own reasons for the advice they offer. They may want to help you make a better decision. Yet they may have their own interests to promote too. So, when someone says, "This is what you ought to do," take a moment to reflect on this advice. Before accepting it at face value, try to think through the actual knowledge, facts, experience, and motives that lie behind the advice.

Mistake No. 95:   *The lawyer created more problems than he solved.*

Lesson: Keep the lawyer(s) under control.

"Although I wasn't in the market to buy a house," says Ramon Williams, "that's exactly what I did. One day I happened to drive by a for-sale-by-owner open house. Just out of curiosity, I decided to go in and take a look. Sure enough, by the end of the afternoon the owners and I had drawn up an agreement. But rather than proceed on our own—

or bring in a real estate agent—we thought it best to consult a lawyer. Unfortunately, the lawyer we went to created more problems than he solved.

"First off, instead of simply formalizing our agreement, the lawyer sided with the seller. It turned out they had both played football (in different years) at the same Dallas high school. For at least the first hour of our two-hour office conference, the seller and the lawyer talked Texas football.

"After that, the lawyer offered his unsolicited opinion that the seller was not getting a good price for his home, and then tried to rewrite other terms where we had already reached an agreement. By the time the conference ended, the cordial relations the seller and I had originally developed were quickly moving toward hostility. The seller wanted to revise, I wanted to carry through our original intent.

"The point was that we had a written and signed agreement. We didn't go to the lawyer for advice about what either of us should have done. We just wanted him to make sure the language we used in our agreement actually meant what we had wanted it to mean.

"Eventually our basic agreement held with just a couple of more concessions on my part. Then the seller and I left the meeting by instructing the lawyer to redraft our final agreement in legalese. The contract came back okay, but our surprise came when we got the bill of $1,050. Seven hours of billing at $150 an hour including the hour wasted on talk of Texas football. At least at this point the seller and I agreed. The bill was outrageous."

Ramon Williams's bad experience with the lawyer who handled his home-buying transaction is not unusual. As evidenced by the wide proliferation of lawyer jokes, record numbers of complaints to bar associations, and increasing attorney malpractice cases, consumer satisfaction with lawyers has reached an all-time low. In fact, former Chief Justice of the United States Warren Burger has even charged that half of the lawyers practicing before the U.S. Supreme Court are incompetent.

So if you choose to bring a lawyer into your home-buying transaction, you should guard against three widespread problems: overbilling, an underqualified lawyer, and gratuitous advice.

When discussing fees with a lawyer, don't just focus on his or her hourly rate. Get a firm estimate of the total bill. In my own dealings with lawyers, I've found that some bill eight hours for the same work another lawyer could perform in two. I once hired a lawyer to answer a question. He billed for 12 hours of research and still couldn't answer the question. When I consulted another attorney, I got the right answer in less than 30 minutes—no research required.

Also make sure your lawyer routinely handles the type of problems you're presenting. Divorce lawyers may know next to nothing about real estate contracts, escrow, and title insurance. Verify the lawyer's successful experience in home-buying transactions.

Beware of gratuitous advice. Many lawyers love to talk and give their opinions regardless of whether they know what they are talking about. I was once in a mortgage closing where in response to a buyer's question the attorney began to explain the mortgage interest figures on the settlement sheet. But rather than admit he didn't know how to calculate mortgage interest, the lawyer tried to bluff his way through. On other occasions I've listened to lawyers give (unsolicited and incorrect) advice about sales prices, investment returns, zoning ordinances, neighborhood desirability, and a myriad of other things.

Several years back a real estate lawyer hired me to perform a market analysis for some land he had bought recently on which he planned to build a small shopping center. To his dismay, though, the lawyer soon learned that the steep grade of the site would have made a shopping center development prohibitively expensive. In this case, the lawyer had "advised" himself about commercial site selection, and that advice cost him over $200,000.

Good lawyers should understand the area of the law where you need help. But they also should know what they do not know. Further, they should not give advice that extends beyond their own experience and expertise. Just as important, don't make the mistake of asking lawyers for opinions in areas outside their competence and experience. Even lawyers with the best intentions have trouble resisting that temptation.

Mistake No. 96: *We shouldn't have taken escrow allowances for repairs.*

Lesson: If you're buying a home that needs extensive repairs, get a substantial price discount.

When you're looking at a home that needs work, you can get the sellers to credit you with an escrow allowance, bargain for a price discount, or maybe go for a combination escrow allowance and price discount. What you should not do, though, is accept an escrow allowance or price discount that exactly matches the estimated costs of repairs. You want substantially more. The chance for underestimates is just too great.

"We knew the house needed work when we bought it," says Kay Schall. "So we got an estimate for repairs before we placed a contract on the home. In total, everything came to around $13,000. To offset these repairs, we wrote a clause into our offer where the sellers would credit us $13,000 at closing. Unfortunately, this escrow allowance didn't come close to covering the repairs we've had to make. So far we've spent $26,136 with the end still not in sight. We now know what it means to own a 'money pit.'"

Kay Schall and her husband made a common mistake. By accepting an escrow allowance for the estimated cost of repairs, they assumed the risk that the repairs could actually be completed for the amount of the estimate. For small repairs, the risk of underestimate may not be too great. But for more extensive work, no contractor can really tell for sure how much money repairs will cost. Here are some of the unexpected problems the Schalls ran up against.

- Previous owners of the house had remodeled it without building permits or city inspections. As a result, before permits could be issued for the new work, the old work had to be inspected. That meant opening up walls so the inspector could see whether the earlier construction had been performed according to code. It hadn't. Therefore, the old remodeling had to be redone.

- Next, the inspector turned his attention to the fireplace in the living room. It, too, had to be completely rebuilt because it had wood instead of metal framing. A second fireplace in the dining room had to be sealed up permanently because of problems with the chimney.

- A wood patio deck had to be torn out because it was built without proper termite barriers between it and the ground.

- A tiled exterior entrance to the home had to be jackhammered to oblivion and then rebuilt with poured concrete with steps of a new height and width to comply with the building code.

- Not only did the whole roof need to be reshingled, much of the wood had to be replaced, and in an area above the old remodeling, the roof had to be raised a foot.

THE CAPUANOS

When Katie and Joe Capuano bought their rundown clapboard home in Stony Brook, Long Island, they figured the age of the house at 60 years and believed they could restore it with a modest amount of work—much of which Joe could do himself. But once the Capuanos got into the restoration project, it became clear that far more work would be necessary than they had anticipated. "Once I started pulling things out, I realized the house was at least 100 years old," says Joe.

By the time they've completed their "modest" restoration, Joe and Katie will have spent more than $55,000 to gut the interior of their house, replace a crumbling foundation and wall beams, add on an extension, and install new siding. "When it's done," says Katie, "it will be everything we could have wanted."

The Capuanos seem to be taking their unexpected expenses with a bit more aplomb than the Schalls. But the experiences of the Schalls and the Capuanos both teach the same lesson: Unless you want to accept the risk of repairs and restoration costs that exceed your estimates, don't accept a dollar-for-dollar escrow allowance or price discount. Instead, build into your figures a large margin for comfort—or require the sellers to make the necessary repairs and improvements before your close your purchase.

Mistake No. 97:   *We accepted an escrow allowance of $6,000 for termite damage. Our repairs cost $18,347.*

Lesson: *All termite inspections are not created equally.*

Before you become a homeowner, most mortgage lenders will require you or the sellers to provide a termite clearance for the house. Generally, a licensed termite inspector comes out, looks around the house with a flashlight, and, at critical points, pokes into the wood with a knife or screwdriver. If no evidence of termites is found, the inspector issues a clearance certificate and sends it to the escrow agent. But if the inspector does find evidence of infestations, he will estimate the cost of treatment and repairs.

Typically, when treatment and repairs are necessary, the sellers either pay for the work or give you an escrow allowance. Which is better? Here you face the same kind of situation as with other kinds of repairs. If the sellers take care of the problem, your risk is reduced. On the other hand, if you accept an escrow credit and can get the work done for a lesser amount, you can come out ahead. The question is, do you want to take a chance?

Ian and Magenta Cordall took a chance and lost. They accepted a $6,000 escrow allowance for termite damage and ended up paying $18,347 for treatment and repairs. "We had no idea," says Ian, "that the inspector's estimates weren't guaranteed. By the time our work was finished, the contractor had to tear out the den and completely rebuild it."

This type of unpleasant surprise occurs because all termite inspections aren't created equal, and even the best ones can miss serious damage.

Primarily, a termite inspection is a sampling process. The inspector pokes here and there hoping to spot any problems that might exist. But there's always the possibility the inspector won't hit the right spot, or the damage may be hidden and relatively inaccessible. Either way actual damage could exceed reported damage. (It's even possible for an infested house to receive a clean bill of health.)

How do you protect yourself?

1. Tag along with the inspector as he tours the house. Did he get under the house and poke around in the crawl space? How about the attic? The foundation? Did he especially check areas where wood (treated or untreated) comes in contact with the ground? How thoroughly has the inspector actually "sampled" the home for termites?

2. Ask the inspector questions. Try to learn the areas of the house that are most vulnerable to infestation. Find out whether other homes in the neighborhood have had a termite problem. See if he discovers any signs that the house has been treated previously. If so, how extensive was the previous damage? Were there any recurrences?

3. If the inspection and treatment results in a warranty, what does it cover? Will it pay for all necessary repairs? Or does it only require the company to re-treat the home with another dose of pesticides?

4. If the company locates infestation and estimates repairs, who bears the risk for underestimates? Is the company merely issuing a good-faith estimate? In that case—unless the firm has been negligent in its inspection—you must pay the repairs if additional damage is found after work begins. Some exterminators, though, guarantee

their estimates. When they miss problems, they'll bear the unanticipated costs to correct them.

What you want to avoid is simply accepting a termite inspection, clearance report, or damage estimate at face value. With some, you can sleep easy knowing you've covered (or limited) your exposure to loss. With others, you just have to hope those pesky little critters have satisfied their appetites somewhere else. Because if they haven't, you'll be the one who's picking up their dinner check.

Mistake No. 98:   *We thought the roof warranty was good for 20 years.*

Lesson: *Carefully determine exactly what types and amounts of repairs your warranties cover.*

"When we bought our house," says Kip Phillips, "the sellers showed us their receipts for a new roof they'd put on four years ago. Plus, they pulled out this engraved certificate that stated in bold print: 20-Year Warranty. With the receipts and the warranty, we didn't think we would have to worry about paying for roof repairs for a long time to come.

"But just 18 months later, the roof started leaking. We learned the shingles were cracking and the entire roof would have to be replaced at a cost of $3,400. At that point, we were really glad we had that 20-year warranty which the owner had transferred to us.

"So, the next thing we did was to contact the shingle manufacturer's local distributor. 'No problem,' he told us, 'we'll send someone out right away to process your claim.' Faithful to his word, several days later a company representative came out to the house. After inspecting the roof, he agreed the shingles needed to be replaced. He then proceeded to write us a check for $600.

"'Six hundred dollars!' we said. 'Replacing that roof is going to cost $3,400. How do you expect us to accept a meager $600?'

"'Because that's the amount the warranty provides,' he said.

"What do you mean?" I asked. "We've got a 20-year warranty."

"'True,' he said, but then pointed to the fine print.

"That's when I knew he might as well have said 'Gottcha.' The fine print stated the company was not liable for the costs of taking off the old roof, installing the new roof, or paying for adhesives, wood repair,

or any other labor or materials. The warranty covered only the pro-
rated cost of the shingles over a 20-year expected life. In other words,
our 20-year roof warranty amounted to nothing more than reimbursement for 70 percent (14/20) of the price of the shingles. To complete
the job, we were still going to be out-of-pocket $2,800."

From this experience, Kip Phillips learned an important (and expensive) lesson: Don't count on warranties to reimburse you for repairs or
replacements unless you've first verified exactly what types of repairs
and amounts of protection the warranty offers. Real estate broker Carl
Steinmetz says his realty firm stopped dealing in home warranties
because "we just had too many cases in which the buyers were discon-
tented with the policy. They always thought it should have covered
something, but then it didn't."

Of course, not everyone agrees with Carl. California Department of
Insurance spokesman John Fogg reports his agency gets fewer complaints about home warranty policies than any other type of insurance.
And the real estate brokerage firm Joan M. Sobeck, Inc., thinks so
highly of warranties that some of its agents buy the policies as a
service to their sellers and buyers. Another broker says, "First-time
buyers often don't know much about fixing up a home. . . . [As a result]
those folks are really drawn to the protection of a warranty."

So what's the bottom line on home warranties? Read the fine print
and look for answers to these questions.

- Does the warranty cover labor, materials, and parts? Or does it just
  apply to certain named items (e.g., roof shingles, furnace combus-
  tion chamber, air conditioner compressor)?

- Will you receive full reimbursement? Or will payments be pro-
  rated?

- Regardless of coverage, will you be required to pay for service
  calls? Some warranties charge homeowners anywhere from $50 to
  $200 each time a repairman is called out to the house.

- If you're buying an existing home with a warranty, ask what items
  are excluded from coverage (e.g., roof, foundation, air conditioner,
  pool equipment, well pump, sprinkler system, plumbing, wiring).

- How long will the warranty last? Most overall warranties with
  existing homes end after one year. New home warranties may
  cover major structural items for 10 years, but limit coverage on
  appliances, furnace, and air conditioner to just one year. (Of course,
  in some instances the manufacturers of these items separately

warrant their quality and performance. So you'll need to check these to determine how you're protected.)

- Does the warranty cover preexisting conditions? If when you buy your home the pipes are rusty or the furnace is clunking and clanging, the warranty may exempt these items from coverage. Many (but not all) warranties only guard against unexpected breakdowns or malfunctions—not sure things. So don't count on a warranty to substitute for a thorough inspection of your home by a professional inspector.

- What is the warranty company's track record for honoring claims? Does it run you through a maze of paperwork and proofs? Or does it enjoy a reputation for fair settlements?

- Is the warranty company in good financial shape? In the past, some homebuyers have lost out on collecting for their claims because the warranty company disappeared or went bankrupt. If you're buying a new home, check to see who stands behind the warranty. Some builders warrant their own work. Others provide protection through independent warranty companies. (HOW is the largest, and has been organized by the National Association of Home Builders.)

    Although you certainly want your builder to stand behind his or her work, in most cases it's better to receive your new home warranty from HOW or another financially strong insurer. Too many builders run into tough financial trouble when housing markets head toward the low point of their up-and-down cycle.

    Also, don't be fooled when builders tell you they've been in business for 25 years. To gauge financial stability, the real question is how long has their present company been in business. Some builders open a company, run it into bankruptcy, and then start another one. Over a period of 20 or 30 years, builders like these may open and close six or eight different firms. Each time they bankrupt a company, they leave their previous homebuyers without a way to collect the claims they may have for defects in their homes.

Overall, during the past 10 years, there's been tremendous growth in home warranty programs. And in general homebuyers, sellers, and builders have all benefited from this trend. But just as with any type of insurance, don't merely assume a warranty will cover your losses. To prevent mistakes, you must understand the fine print.

Mistake No. 99:   *Our homeowners' insurance policy didn't cover the full amount of our losses.*

Lesson: *Don't take your homeowners' insurance for granted. Closely check your coverages.*

When fire swept through the Oakland-Berkeley, California, hills in October 1991, Ron and Betty Bugaj lost their $500,000 home and all their personal belongings. But the Bugajes were not alone. In one of the worst residential firestorms in U.S. history, more than 3,300 other homeowners suffered total losses. As tragic as the fire was, though, for many of these families their troubles were just beginning. "The damage we really suffered," said Betty, "was in our negotiations with the insurance company."

Like more than 1,000 other firestorm victims, the Bugajes learned after the fire that their homeowners' insurance policy would pay far less than they expected. To get the amounts they thought they were entitled to, the Bugajes wrangled back and forth with their insurance company for over 10 months. Adding to their hassle were the $75,000 in legal and consulting fees their negotiations with the insurance company cost them.

In the end, the Bugajes and most of the other firestorm victims did settle with their insurers. But only after the California Department of Insurance, various consumer advocacy groups, and widespread unfavorable publicity pressured the insurance companies to give in. Although to some extent several insurers had tried to lowball their policyholders, most of the settlement problems resulted because homeowners had not purchased the insurance coverage they actually needed (or thought they had).

The important lesson of the Oakland-Berkeley hills firestorm was not that most insurance companies are the bad guys. Rather, it's that far too many homeowners don't actually understand their insurance coverages. They just buy a homeowners' policy and assume (incorrectly) they have the protection they need. This is a big mistake you should avoid.

To make sure your policy adequately protects your home and belongings, ask your insurance agent or check your policy to find the answers to these questions.

What perils are covered? In insurance lingo, a peril is a cause of loss. No insurance policy covers every type of loss. Some policies exclude hurricanes, floods, mudslides, sink holes, earthquakes, and riots. Sometimes freezing pipes and roof collapse due to a buildup of snow and ice are not covered. Apart from war and civil rebellion, though, you can usually buy an endorsement or rider to cover perils that basic policies don't insure.

What property is covered? With tens of millions of Americans now working in their homes, it's important to realize some of your business property or business inventories may not be covered under your homeowners' policy. Nor are your pets, golf cart, or snowmobile. Similarly, if you own any expensive antiques, jewelry, furs, artwork, or a collection of stamps, coins, or baseball cards, you'll want to find out whether they're covered, and, if so, for how much. More than likely you'll have to pay extra to secure adequate protection. If you're a writer, store an extra copy of the manuscript you're working on with friends or in a safe deposit box. (Dozens of writers in the Oakland-Berkeley fire lost computer disks and partially completed books and articles.) Your homeowners' policy won't pay for the value of your past work, or even the market value of a finished manuscript.

How much will the company pay? This issue causes the most problems between homeowners and their insurance companies. Unfortunately, there's lots of room here for confusion and ambiguity.

First, let's consider your house. Generally you can choose either replacement cost coverage or actual cash value coverage. With a replacement cost policy, your insurer agrees to pay you enough to repair or replace your house at today's prices. Under actual cash value coverage, the company subtracts a figure for depreciation from the costs of replacement. Naturally, it's better to have replacement cost coverage. Otherwise, the older your house and the greater its wear and tear, the less you can collect.

However, regardless of which type of coverage you select, here are some questions where misunderstandings frequently occur (as they did in the Oakland-Berkeley fire).

- How much will you be able to collect if you choose not to rebuild?

- What happens if government regulations prevent repairs or rebuilding? (For example, some homes now located in coastal areas, floodplains, wetlands, or hillsides could not be rebuilt because of new safety or environmental regulations.)

- What if new government regulations (safety codes, environmental laws, building regulations) significantly increase the costs to reconstruct (replace) your existing home? In the Oakland fire, many destroyed homes were 30 to 70 years old. Thus, they couldn't be rebuilt as they previously had been built. Extra regulations added as much as $50,000 or more to their rebuilding costs. Yet homeowners' policies often exclude these types of costs because they're not really "replacement" costs. This fact came as a big surprise to many homeowners when they learned that in order to rebuild they were going to have to come up with substantial amounts of cash from their own pockets.

- How much will your policy pay for your home's unique architectural or historical value? (Usually nothing unless you've requested special coverages.)

- If your insurer drags its feet while settling your claim, are you entitled to interest payments on the proceeds when the company does finally pay?

- How much are your policy limits? Regardless of how much it costs to replace your home, the company typically won't pay any more than your policy limits. So make sure you periodically increase the limits of your policy to keep up with rising costs of construction.

- If you choose an actual cash value policy, how will your insurance company calculate depreciation?

It's far better for you to discuss all these questions with your insurance agent before you suffer a loss. After a loss occurs is the wrong time to try to sort out problems in your coverage.

Plus, what is true for your home is also true for your household furniture and personal belongings. To collect as much as possible for the contents of your home, you should choose replacement cost coverage. But keep a list and photographic (or video) inventory of your personal property. Under the terms of your policy, you'll be required to prove your loss. Photos or videos stored in a safe place can serve as good proof of what you owned. Besides, without a detailed inventory of your possessions, chances are you'll forget or overlook a lot of things that you're entitled to collect for.

What liability protection does your policy provide? In addition to protecting your home and its contents, your homeowners' policy will protect you against lawsuits. Typically this provides "slip and fall" coverage where someone is injured on your property. It may also cover you for things like running into someone on your bicycle or hitting someone with a golf ball with your mean slice.

If you live in a condominium, townhouse, or subdivision development where you're a member of a homeowners' association, check to see what type of liability coverage the association carries. In some states, you can be held personally liable (along with other homeowners) when someone is negligently injured on the common areas of the property (swimming pool, bike trails, tennis courts, clubhouse, hallways).

According to attorney Benny Kass, who's a specialist in condominium and homeowners' association law, too many community associations "are pitifully underinsured and represent a significant risk to association members."

How much are the premiums? Apart from fully understanding your insurance coverages, before you offer to buy a home, you should determine how much adequate protection will cost you. In recent years property insurance companies and homeowners have suffered billions of dollars in losses (Hurricane Andrew, the Oakland-Berkeley firestorm, the Los Angeles riots, the Midwest floods, the Los Angeles-Malibu fires). As a result, some companies have raised their premiums and made insurance much more difficult to obtain in some areas with high loss potential.

In Florida after Hurricane Andrew, for example, many major insurance companies canceled tens of thousands of homeowner policies, and several insurers tried to withdraw completely from writing policies in hurricane areas. In response, the Florida legislature passed a six-month moratorium on policy cancellations. At present, no one can predict how all these troubles will work themselves out. But for these and other reasons, it does mean homebuyers and homeowners will need to check their coverages and their premiums very closely. You can't assume that you'll be able to get the coverages you need at a price you can afford.

Mistake No. 100: *After we bought the house, our property taxes jumped by $1,200 and we got hit with a $600 special assessment for new sidewalks.*

Lesson: *Prior to buying, find out how your property taxes will be calculated.*

When Stan and Beth Hill bought their home, the information sheet their Realtor gave them listed property taxes for the most recent year at $1,700. Shortly after the Hills bought, however, their taxes shot up to $2,900. In addition, the city notified Stan and Beth that it was installing new sidewalks throughout their neighborhood. Their share of these costs would total $600, and that amount would also be added to the Hills' tax bill for the coming year.

In looking to the past rather than the future, Stan and Beth made a common mistake. They assumed their property taxes would cost about the same as the sellers had been paying. But in many cities and counties throughout the United States, you can't make that assumption.

Under the laws in most states, county assessors periodically estimate a home's value for the purpose of levying property taxes. The period for reassessment, though, might be annual, quadrennial, whenever the assessor's office gets around to it, or sometimes when a property is sold and a new deed (and sales price) is recorded in the county records. In addition, in many areas homeowners are entitled to various exemptions (homestead, mortgage, senior citizen). So even when two homes are assessed at the same value and the valuations are current, the property taxes can vary greatly.

In Stan and Beth's case, their property tax surprise arose for two reasons. First, the home had not been reassessed for four years, and during that period values in the neighborhood had increased about 35 percent. Second, seven years earlier the sellers had built on a new 800-square-foot master bedroom suite that enhanced the home's value but had not been noticed by the tax assessor.

As a result, on the books at the courthouse, the home carried an assessed value of only $106,300. But when the Hill's purchase price of $179,000 came through the records office, it triggered an immediate reassessment of the home's current market value. The property taxes on the Hills' home went up by over 60 percent.

To prevent this type of surprise, you should learn the ins and outs of the property tax system and procedures in your area. If the home you're planning to buy is underassessed, or if the sellers qualify for more exemptions than you are entitled to, you might see a steep rise in your property tax bill.

On the other hand, by learning the ins and outs of property taxes in your area, you might also discover an overassessment. In recent years some homes in the Northeast, California, Florida, Oklahoma, Texas, Arizona, and several other states have sold for less than their peak prices of earlier years. So their current market values may have fallen below their assessed value. When that's the case, you can expect to see your property taxes fall.

Overall, here are some of the property tax questions you should discuss with your real estate agent or the tax assessors office.

- What is the current market value of the home you're buying?
- What is the current assessed value of the home? (In some tax jurisdictions, the assessed value is stated as a percentage of the home's market value. Therefore, you should look at both the tax assessor's appraised valued and the assessed value before you conclude a home is underassessed.)
- After you buy, can you expect the *assessed* value of the home to increase, decrease, or remain about the same?
- Are you entitled to any exemptions that can reduce your property tax bill?
- What is the local millage rate? (One mill equals a thousandth of a dollar. A millage rate of say, 17, would mean a property tax of $17 for every $1,000 of assessed value.)
- Will any improvements you plan to make to the home increase its assessed value? (Some types of improvements will add significantly to your assessed value—if the tax assessor learns about them. Built-ins, room additions, a swimming pool, or wall-to-wall carpeting, for example, typically increase a home's assessed value. A new roof, furnace, or hot water heater may not. Every tax assessor's office has its own way of operating. You'll have to check for the specifics as they may apply to the home you buy.)
- What amount of taxes can you expect to pay? (To calculate this figure, you need to multiply the millage rate expressed as a decimal times the home's expected assessed value. Seventeen mills, for example, converts to .017. With an assessed value of $100,000, your property taxes would run $1,700 a year.)

SPECIAL ASSESSMENTS

In addition to property taxes, from time to time the government may levy special assessments. These charges usually pay for new sidewalks, sewers, sewage disposal plants, street widenings, parks, or other types of "infrastructure." In most cases special assessments will range between $300 and $1,000. But on occasion they can go as high as $2,000 or $3,000, or even more.

Since special assessments can upset a budget, you should try to find out whether any lie on the horizon for your neighborhood. Plus, it's a good idea to learn of proposed "infrastructure" changes before you buy. Better parks may add to your home's value. But widening the street through your neighborhood or in front of your home could bring more traffic and take away from the value of your home.

Mistake No. 101: *We didn't know title insurance companies offered discount policies.*

Lesson: *Before you set up escrow, ask whether the sellers have a title policy that can be transferred to you and your lender. It could save you money.*

One of the most important steps in your home-buying process will be the title search. Before you and your lender release funds to the sellers, you'll want to verify that they actually own the property and that any outstanding liens or claims against the home will be taken care of prior to closing.

Years ago most title searches were performed by attorneys, who would then offer an opinion whether title to the home was marketable ("free and clear"). Although still common in some areas of the country, most lenders and homebuyers today no longer use attorneys to assure title. Instead, they buy a title insurance policy.

When an attorney makes a mistake or otherwise misses a defect in the home's title, the only way you can make him or her pay for your losses is to hire another lawyer to sue the first one. That's an expensive, time-consuming, and uncertain proposition. With title insurance, though, the insurance company agrees to pay the legal expenses necessary to defend the title to your home against other claims. If unsuccessful in its defense, the company will pay for you and your lender's losses.

Of course, like all insurers, title companies write their policies with various exceptions and limitations. For example, if your next-door neighbor's garage sits a foot onto your side of the property line at the time you bought your home, the insurer may exclude that known problem from its coverage. Also, some basic title policies cover only the lender. Adding your name to the policy may cost slightly more.

In general, title insurance has proved itself to be a wise purchase for most homebuyers. It dramatically reduces the possibility that you'll be drawn into a long, drawn-out legal battle when some ex-wife of a long-ago owner shows up and claims her ex-husband forged her name to the deed when he sold the house as part of their divorce settlement. For most homebuyers, it is a mistake not to buy title insurance.

Once a decision to buy is made, though, other mistakes are common. The first is that many homebuyers don't realize title companies offer two types of coverages: lender's policies and owner's policies. As mentioned earlier, to protect your equity in the property, you (or the sellers) may need to pay an additional premium. Also, you might inquire whether you can obtain increasing amounts of protection as your home appreciates in value. Title policies last for as long as you own your home, but most policies limit coverage to your home's original purchase price.

Second, many homebuyers do not know they should find out whether the sellers of the home have a title policy that can be updated and transferred to them. If your sellers do have title coverage, by sticking with the same company you might be able to save several hundred dollars. If you (or the sellers) can't save money that way, you should compare insurance premiums among title companies. In some states these premiums are set by law, so you won't find any differences among companies. But many states have moved toward increasing competition, and shopping around can pay off.

Third, title problems on the way to closing are becoming increasingly common. With so many bank and S&L failures, as well as the huge volume of home mortgages being traded among lenders in the secondary market like baseball cards, the paper trail for existing liens and previous mortgage satisfactions sometimes can prove cumbersome to follow. So stay on top of your lender (or attorney) to see that all the necessary title paperwork is getting processed in a timely manner.

On occasion, loan officers or loan processors busy themselves with credit reports, document verifications, and the appraisal, and leave the title search and property survey to the last minute. When problems then crop up, closing has to be delayed, which disrupts moving plans for both buyers and sellers. Although most title defects and boundary disputes can be straightened out, often doing so can take several weeks to several months. In general, good planning and timely processing of the paperwork can keep you and the sellers free from the type of troublesome situation.

Mistake No. 102: *Our closing was like showdown at the Great Western corral.*

Lesson: The best closing is a no-surprises closing.

Most mortgage closings go smoothly. On occasion, though, lack of preparation or last-minute changes can create turmoil. "We felt it was a bad sign," says Wendy Kantor, "when the real estate agent telephoned us two days before closing and told us the sellers had decided to take the refrigerator and window air conditioners with them. However, these items were already included in our purchase price. So the agent said the sellers would give us a credit for their value and we could work out the details at closing.

"But at closing, the sellers only wanted to give us $500. That figure wasn't acceptable to us. We thought $1,000, maybe even $1,250 was closer to the mark. Besides that, we found a $600 mistake in the addition in the closing statement and another $1,300 in garbage fees that we hadn't expected. By the time that closing finally settled, it was like showdown at the Great Western corral."

I can empathize with Wendy because I once went through a mortgage closing disaster much like hers—only I was the seller. In my case, several days before closing my agent telephoned and said the buyers had come up short on cash and asked whether I would be willing to carry back $2,000 in seller financing. I said no. Since I was moving out of town, I didn't want to worry about collecting $2,000 from a distance of 1,200 miles. If the buyers didn't pay, I could end up spending more than $2,000 in lawyer's bills just to collect.

However, once we got into closing, the buyers proceeded on the assumption I was going to help them with their financing. As I later learned, my agent had set us up. He figured that once we were sitting in closing—both of us with loaded moving vans—we would be forced to work out some kind of compromise. And that's what we did.

But from that experience, I learned the same lesson Wendy Kantor learned: Make sure all the details of the transaction are known and agreed upon by all parties prior to closing. In fact, to avoid these kinds of last-minute showdowns, many mortgage loans and home-buying transactions are closed by escrow without buyers, sellers, agents, lender, and attorneys all meeting together around a conference table. I've been involved in both types of closings and definitely favor the escrow approach.

Nevertheless, even with in absentia escrow closings, you still must carefully check the figures on your closing statement to make sure they're totaled correctly and that the lender hasn't thrown in some "garbage fees" that were not properly disclosed to you in the lender's good-faith Real Estate Settlement and Procedures Act (RESPA) disclosure statement. Plus, stay alert for last-minute pressure tactics to renegotiate your transaction in the other party's favor. Some unethical sellers (buyers) or their attorneys use this technique to force concessions they otherwise couldn't get. This is another example where forewarned is forearmed.

Mistake No. 103: *We couldn't believe the way the sellers left the house for us.*

Lesson: *If at all possible, arrange a final walk-through and inspection of the house before settlement—and ideally after the sellers have moved out.*

"We couldn't believe the mess," recalls Derek Chapman. "We walked into the house the day after settlement and discovered the sellers had left piled-up boxes of trash throughout the house, the inside of the oven looked like a grease pit, the carpeting and floors were all tracked up with mud (evidently from their movers), and the dining room chandelier was missing. We also learned the den did not have hardwood floors as we thought.

"When we first looked at the house," Derek continued, "the sellers had a large area rug in the den so all we saw was the hardwood floors around the edge of the room. Naturally we assumed the floor under the rug was also finished hardwood. But it wasn't. That part of the floor was unfinished pine. I guess we should have pulled back the rug just to make sure. But it really wasn't anything I had even seen before—or would have imagined."

Derek Chapman's experience teaches several lessons. First, don't assume. When you're inspecting a house, get nosy. Pull back rugs, open the cabinets, drawers, and the oven door. Look behind pictures or other wall hangings. Maybe even look under the furniture. It's better to discover flaws, stains, cracks, or unfinished floors before you make your offer rather than after.

Second, if at all possible, schedule settlement after the sellers have moved out. Then prior to closing, do a final walk-through and inspection. You want to learn whether the sellers have left the home in satisfactory condition and that they have not taken any personal property, appliances, or fixtures that were supposed to stay with the house. Inspecting a vacant house also gives you another chance to discover any defects that were previously hidden by the sellers' selective placement of furniture, area rugs, or wall hangings.

It's far easier to work out problems before the sellers have received their money than it is after they've deposited their settlement check. This is especially true when the sellers are moving out of town. Once the sellers are gone with their money, as a practical matter, you don't have much leverage. You might be able to sue, but that will nearly always cost you more time, hassle, and money than you could ever hope to collect.

If you can't do a final walk-through before the settlement and after the sellers' move date, you might consider putting a clause in your purchase offer whereby 10 percent (or so) of the sellers' sales proceeds are escrowed until you've had time to check out the house.

As another tactic, you might put a compulsory arbitration clause in your purchase agreement. With this kind of clause, you and the sellers use an arbitrator to settle disputes instead of a lawsuit. As you might expect, lawyers often advise against compulsory arbitration because it cuts down on legal fees. From most buyers' perspective, though, saving on lawyer's bills and court costs stands as an advantage, not a disadvantage. Through arbitration, you also can settle your disputes much quicker than with a lawsuit. Arbitration may not be right for everyone, but it's definitely a method of resolving disagreements that you should consider.

Of course, your overall goal is to avoid lawsuits, arbitration, and disagreements with the sellers. And you can go a long way toward reducing these possibilities by a final walk-through of the house.

NEWLY BUILT HOMES

When it comes to new homes, "don't make the mistake of assuming without asking," cautions William Young, who serves as director of consumer affairs for the National Association of Home Builders. Mr. Young's advice is aimed at buyers of new homes who expect their homes will include all the same amenities and custom features they've seen in their builder's model homes. But as homeowner Paul Jakulski discovered, that's seldom the case.

Paul was conducting a preclosing walk-through of his newly built $185,000 split-level ranch home when he discovered that, unlike the model homes he was shown, his home lacked skylights, which were very important to him. "Without the skylights," Paul complained to the builder, "the house is way too dark."

The builder sympathized with Paul but pointed out that in their contract, skylights were optional and not included in the basic price. Since Paul hadn't specified he wanted them, the builder didn't put them in. To do so now that the home was virtually complete would cost twice as much as if they had been installed during the construction process.

Unfortunately, Paul's mistake happens all too frequently. So if you plan to buy a new home that's not yet completed, you'll want to check two things: First, don't assume those gold-plated bathroom fixtures or the marble fireplaces in the den and master bedroom are standard features. Read your purchase contract closely. Look for those magic words optional or upgrades. With some houses it's the upgrades and options that transform the frog into Prince Charming.

Second, keep tabs on the construction process throughout the period your home is being built. Don't wait until final walk-through to discover the features you wanted aren't the features you're getting. Even when you've accurately listed your options and upgrades, builders and contractors can make mistakes.

In addition, if you decide on changes during construction (as you undoubtedly will), make them as early as you can and put them in writing. The earlier you specify changes, the less it will cost you. And memories are too fragile and building sites too hectic to rely on ad hoc talks with your builder, a sales representative, or a contractor. Whether buying a new home or an existing home, good communication is one important key to a no-surprises home-buying experience.

Mistake No. 104: *The sellers wouldn't move out of the house.*

Lesson: Put a penalty clause in your contract that will force the sellers either to move or pay.

"A funny thing happened when first-time buyers Janie Brown and Paul Kelley showed up with a bottle of champagne at their new home in La Mesa. The sellers refused to move out." So reports Marsha Kay Seff in the *San Diego Tribune*. But according to Marsha, Janie and Paul kept their spirits up, put the champagne back in the refrigerator, and after two weeks of legal process, proceeded to evict the sellers.

Surprising as it may seem, sellers (or tenants) who refuse to move after buyers have closed on a house is not all that uncommon. Take the case of Chauntann Reid. Pooling money contributed by several of her brothers and sisters, Chauntann decided to buy a bargain-priced home at a sheriff's foreclosure sale. After learning the ins and outs of how foreclosure auctions work, Chauntann submitted a successful bid for a two-story brick row house with garage. This lucky new homeowner, though, soon found out that buying a foreclosed home can be easier than moving into it.

Not only did the prior owner of the home challenge the validity of the foreclosure sale, she filed bankruptcy. Both these legal actions stalled any eviction proceedings that Chauntann could have used to take possession of the home.

Five months have now passed since she became a homeowner, but Chauntann and her three children are still living with her sister. With mounting legal fees, property tax bills, and sewer charges that Chauntann must pay to protect her ownership interest in the house, she can't afford to move out and rent her own apartment.

Getting a tenant out of a house you've bought can present more difficulties than removing reluctant sellers. As a matter of law, a tenant's lease takes priority over the possession rights of a new owner. If the tenant's rental agreement with the previous owners still has six months to run, then the tenants have the right to stay in the home for six more months (as long as they pay the rent, of course).

Even when the tenants don't have the security of a lease, they may have the protection of various pro-tenant ordinances. Some cities require property owners to give tenants 60 or 90 days' notice, sometimes longer, before they can be forced to move. Similarly, if a tenant is pregnant or files bankruptcy, the law may offer special protection against eviction.

To guard against sellers who won't move, you can put a clause in your purchase contract that obligates the sellers to pay $100 a day (or whatever) for each day they stay beyond the date they're supposed to move out. That type of penalty generally encourages sellers to quickly find someplace else to live.

If you buy a foreclosed home with the "owners" still living there, be aware of the risks. You may be in for a long and expensive legal battle to evict them.

Likewise, should you plan to buy a home that's occupied by tenants, find out the terms of their rental agreement. (It may not make any difference whether the agreement is oral or written.) Then verify the tenants' intentions and planned moving date. Also, check with a lawyer or the local landlord-tenant regulatory agency to see if the tenants are protected against eviction by any laws or regulations. Whatever you do, though, don't simply assume that because you're the owner of the house you have rights of possession. Strange as it may seem, that's not the way the law necessarily operates.

NEW HOMES

Unless squatters have moved in, you're not likely to have any problems with reluctant tenants if you buy a new home. But new home buyers sometimes experience another kind of problem that keeps them from moving into their home as scheduled. Construction of the home may not be completed. Delays in completing a home can result because of bad weather, shortages of building supplies, labor strikes, excessive change orders, or foot dragging by the builder, contractor, or subcontractor.

Although you should be somewhat tolerant with your builder, nevertheless you also might want to include a completion delay penalty in your purchase contract. I know of new homebuyers who have had to wait anywhere from two to six months beyond the completion date they were promised. With a delay that long, you should expect a penalty payment if the builder or his contractors are responsible.

More than likely, though, you'll have to negotiate tough to get it. As a rule, builders don't like penalty clauses. But if you're committing to move on a set date, your builder should commit to having a home ready for you to move into. If within a reasonable grace period he or she can't meet that commitment, the builder should pay the price of your inconvenience and alternative housing arrangements.

Conclusion

The Biggest Mistakes of All

Mistake No. 105: We didn't buy because we were afraid of making a mistake.

Lesson: *Educate yourself. But don't let fear block your goal of home ownership.*

Kyle and Shannon Marks have been shopping for a home for more than two years. Instead of buying, though, they've continued to rent. Everytime they get close to making an offer, they let their worries overwhelm their ambition. "You can never be too cautious," says Shannon. "Our home will probably be the biggest investment we ever make. We certainly don't want to make a mistake."

Granted, throughout this book I've emphasized the need to antici-pate and prevent mistakes in home buying. As you now know, home buying has become more complex and there are lots of ways to go wrong. Nevertheless, one of the biggest mistakes of all is to perpetu-ally put off becoming a homeowner because you fear making a mis-take. Educate yourself. Shop the market. Get reliable advice from knowledgeable experts. But don't needlessly avoid making a commit-ment.

"You can sit on the fence forever. Eventually, though, the parade goes by," advises corporate relocation executive Keith Bisogno. Or in the words of country singer Billy Ray Cyrus, "dreams move on if you wait too long."

Yes, it does pay to exercise caution and good judgment. Yet contrary to Shannon Marks's belief, you can be too cautious. To get ahead in life, you've got to move from the rational and cautious to a "leap of faith." In fact, an excessive fear of making a mistake is itself irrational. As mentioned earlier, decision expert Theodore Rubin frequently points out that no decision is ever perfect. To a large extent, a successful decision results not just from the decision itself. It results from your commitment to make the decision work for you.

"If I compare my house to an imaginary dream house," writes Dr. Rubin, "my house comes off poorly and I destroy any chance of enjoying it. On the other hand, if I compare my house to houses that actually exist, it may come off well in terms of any real specifications a home requires to be comfortable. This is a true luxury, one I can appreciate in reality."

Quite often, people who put off buying a home out of fear of making a mistake are really fearful of making a decision and then committing to that decision. They keep holding out for a home that has no flaws, no shortcomings, or no drawbacks. But, of course, such a home doesn't exist. If you find yourself falling into that trap, put yourself back on the right path by asking and answering these questions.

- Have you really thought through and ranked your priorities? Have you discovered your most important feelings and values? Are you permitting the opinions and views of others to conflict with or overshadow your own priorities? You can't "have it all," nor can you satisfy everybody. Keep focused on what's most important to you.

- Are you comparing houses and neighborhoods with an open mind? Have you fully explored your options and possibilities? Have you educated yourself about alternative home finance plans, neighborhoods, types of homes, and price ranges?

  To exercise good judgment, you need a good view of what the market offers. Put your creativity to work. You shouldn't let wishful thinking push aside market realities. But neither should you necessarily accept fewer choices than you actually have. Education and creative thinking can go a long way toward reducing your fear, anxiety, frustration, or disappointment.

- Do you see various possibilities and options as problems or opportunities? Too often, fear creates negative thinking. Within a context of negative thinking, it's easy to let yourself get bogged down by anxiety and hopelessness. You may think, "We'll never be able to find what we're looking for." Or maybe you'll tell yourself, "We can't find anything we like that we can afford."

Fear and negative thinking often go together and block your ability to create choices, options, or possibilities that could work for you. You may resign yourself to renting—or you could jump into a decision "just to get it over with."

On the other hand, when you try to frame your options in more positive terms, you'll develop more self-confidence. As you develop a here's-what-we-can-do attitude, you turn fear and resignation into eagerness and excitement. Where fear can generate avoidance and hold you back, optimism and a positive outlook can help you see opportunity and commit to action. You'll not only make a good decision, you'll make that decision work for you.

Mistake No. 106: We've thought it over and decided to continue renting.

Lesson: *For the great majority of Americans, continuing to rent will prove to be the greatest mistake of all.*

During the past several years I've seen hundreds of newspaper and magazine articles that warn against buying a home. "These are uncertain times," the articles say. "Buying a home is no longer the sure thing it once was. A renter who invests wisely may well come out ahead of those who buy."

Poppycock. Apart from the fact naysaying "experts" have been wrong in their warnings against buying for at least the past 50 years (see Chapter 2), a look at three simple reasons shows why home ownership beats renting:

1. Home ownership produces the safest and surest opportunity to build personal wealth.

2. Over the course of a lifetime, Americans who own will spend far less money on housing than those who rent.

3. Home ownership yields transcendental benefits that can far outstrip the financial returns.

BUILD PERSONAL WEALTH

With inflation rates (at least for now) sitting well below the big increases in the Consumer Price Index we experienced in the late 1970s and early 1980s, the notion has taken hold that home ownership will no longer produce good financial returns. Supposedly, you're better off investing in the stock market. Of course, in terms of rate of return, the fallacy behind that idea can be exposed easily (See Mistake No. 20). However, even more important than rate of return stands the opportunity home ownership offers to build personal wealth.

In fact, a recent report released by Harvard University's Joint Center for Housing Studies has found that after allowing for differences in age and income, on average, Americans who owned their own homes enjoyed net worths 20 to 40 times greater than those who rented. Without a doubt, home equity makes up the single largest source of Americans' personal wealth.

A relatively few people may strike it rich in the stock market. But for millions of others the stock market means high risk and high losses. On the other hand, building wealth through increasing home equity has consistently proven to be the safest and surest route to a personal net worth of six figures or more. When you combine a decreasing mortgage balance with even modest rates of home appreciation, your wealth multiplies.

Take a close look at the three examples in Table C.1. These figures reveal how your wealth will grow over time with a beginning down payment of just $10,000 on a home priced at $100,000 and selected appreciation rates of 3, 5, and 7 percent.

As Table C.1 shows, even with only a 3 percent average annual rate of appreciation, your beginning home equity of $10,000 will grow to more than $128,301 within 20 years. And by retirement age you would have accumulated home equity of $326,200. Plus, remember, these gains in equity and personal wealth (unlike stock market investments) will have built up free of local, state, or federal income taxes.

Now, don't get me wrong. I'm not trying to persuade you against investing in the stock market, bond funds, mutual funds, or even commercial real estate, precious art, or antiques. On the contrary, I agree with financial advisors who encourage individuals and families to develop a diversified investment portfolio. Most people should not put all their eggs into one basket. However, diversification can come later. As a starting point, first become a homeowner.

Growing Home Equity at 3% Annual Home Appreciation

	Years of Ownership			
	10	20	30	40
Appreciated home value	$134,300	$180,600	$242,700	$326,200
Outstanding mortgage balance	77,679	52,299	00	00
Home equity	56,620	128,301	242,700	326,200

Growing Home Equity at 5% Annual Home Appreciation

	Years of Ownership			
	10	20	30	40
Appreciated home value	$162,870	$265,330	$432,190	$704,000
Outstanding mortgage balance	77,679	52,299	00	00
Home equity	85,211	213,031	432,190	704,000

Growing Home Equity at 7% Annual Home Appreciation

	Years of Ownership			
	10	20	30	40
Appreciated home value	$196,720	$386,970	$761,230	$1,497,400
Outstanding mortgage balance	77,679	52,299	00	00
Home equity	119,041	334,671	761,230	1,497,400

Table C.1   Building Wealth with Home Equity[1]
[1]Assumes a $100,000 home purchase price bought with a $10,000 down payment and an original mortgage of $90,000 at 7.25 interest over 30 years.

HOMEOWNERS SPEND LESS FOR HOUSING THAN RENTERS

Aside from accumulating wealth through home equity, homeowners build more wealth than renters for another reason. Homeowners typically spend less for housing than renters. Although the exact cost advantages will differ among the various towns and cities throughout the United States, over time and in general, rents will continue to increase as mortgage payments remain the same (or increase only to a capped amount). Then after your mortgage is paid off, your payments fall to zero.

This cost advantage of owning, then, means that as homeowners grow older, they have more money left from their paychecks after paying for housing. So, they'll have more money to invest. Look at how rents and mortgage payments compare over time (Figure C.1).

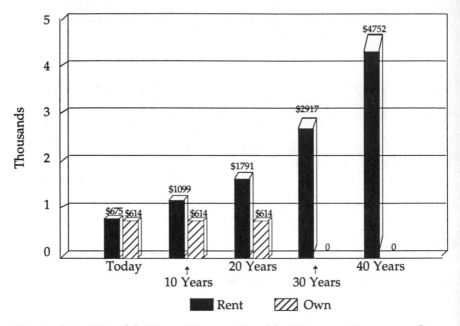

Figure C.1 Monthly Rents Versus Monthly Mortgage Payments Over Time[1]

[1]Mortgage payments are based on a 30-year, fixed-rate mortgage at 7.25 percent in the amount of $90,000. Rents begin at $675 per month and increase 5 percent per year.

Based on the example monthly mortgage payments and rent levels shown here, you can see that within 10 years renters will pay substantially more each month for housing than homeowners. After 20 or 30 years, renters (if they can afford them) will be paying thousands more *per month* than homeowners. If homeowners invested an average of only $1,000 a month of these cost savings, say over years 10 through 40, they will accumulate (assuming an annual return of 5 percent) approximately $675,000. That wealth, of course, is in addition to the equity they will have built up in their homes.

There's simply no question that the housing cost savings that homeowners enjoy as they grow older gives them a powerful advantage over renters in their ability to generate personal wealth and create a diversified investment portfolio. But don't just take the figures here or even the results of the previously mentioned Harvard study at face value. Test this conclusion for yourself. Compare the wealth position of renters and homeowners you know who have reached their 40s, 50s, or 60s. I'm sure you'll find that the net worth of your older friends and relatives who own their own homes greatly exceeds the wealth of those who have remained long-term renters.

HOME OWNERSHIP YIELDS TRANSCENDENTAL BENEFITS

"Hey, we own this. This home is ours," says Melanie Watts. "We never thought of our home as a money machine—although our equity has steadily built up and our payments are lower now than when we first bought 12 years ago. We became homeowners because we wanted the feelings you get when you own instead of rent. I can't describe it, but it's real.

"After owning our own home, I don't think we could ever feel comfortable again as tenants. In fact, our next plan is to buy a few rental houses and let our tenants put their money into our retirement fund.

"I guess what I'm saying," Melanie continued, "is that the financial returns of ownership are great. But the most important benefit of owning is ownership itself. There's nothing like knowing at least a small part of this big old world belongs to you.

"Ownership gives me feelings of security and comfort. When I rented I never felt in control of my life. Now I do. To us, at least, home ownership and ownership of property is a transcendental experience. I'm not into Zen or anything like that. But I do believe anyone who rents is missing one of the best feelings they can have. Although we intend to become landlords and will need tenants, I still believe most people who continue to rent are making a big mistake."

History shows Melanie is right. Failing to become a homeowner remains the most common and most costly mistake of all.

Index